Plain Style

Other Books by Christopher Lasch

The American Liberals and the Russian
Revolution (1962)

The New Radicalism in America (1965)

The Agony of the American Left (1969)

The World of Nations (1973)

Haven in a Heartless World (1977)

The Culture of Narcissism (1979)

The Minimal Self (1984)

The True and Only Heaven (1991)

The Revolt of the Elites and the Betrayal
of Democracy (1995)

Women and the Common Life (1997)
(edited by Elisabeth Lasch-Quinn)

10   9   8   7   6   5   4   3   2   1

Published by
University of Pennsylvania Press
Philadelphia, Pennsylvania 19104-4011

LIBRARY OF CONGRESS CATALOGING-IN-PUBLICATION DATA

Lasch, Christopher.
    1. Plain style : a guide to written English / Christopher Lasch ; edited
and with an introduction by Stewart Weaver.
        p. cm.
    Includes index.
    ISBN 0-8122-3673-4 (alk. paper) —
    ISBN 0-8122-1814-0 (paper : alk. paper)
    1. English language—Rhetoric.   2. English language—Grammar.
3. English language—Style.   I. Weaver, Stewart Angas.   II. Title.
PE1408 .L3195   2002
808'.042—dc21

                                                        2002019163

Plain Style

A Guide to Written English

Christopher Lasch

Edited and with an introduction by
Stewart Weaver

PENN

UNIVERSITY OF PENNSYLVANIA PRESS

PHILADELPHIA

. . . THE WHICH I shall endeavor to manifest in a plain style with singular regard unto the simple truth in all things.

—William Bradford, *History of Plymouth Plantation* (c. 1650)

WHEN IT IS my purpose to Teach, I think I should not say that in two words which may be said in one. . . . That key is to be chosen which doth open best, although it be of wood, if there be not a golden key of the same efficacy.

—William Ames, *The Marrow of Sacred Divinity* (1643)

THE SCIENCE OF correct Writing having been a Subject exhausted by so many able Hands, and seeing all the Rabble of Scribblers are such indisputable Proficients in it; not to mention my own Incapacity for such an Undertaking; I shall not be so vain as to offer my Thoughts upon it: But I shall apply my Labours at this Time, to an Ornament of a contrary Nature, which is a Theme entirely New, Namely, *The Art of Writing Incorrectly*. . . . If this false Taste prevails amongst us, we shall quickly prove such a Generation of Blusterers, that our Country will resemble the Cave of *Aeolus*, where the Winds make their General Rendezvous, and battle and clash together in an eternal Din and Uproar. For my own Part, I look upon it to be the Duty of every one, as far as in him lies, to lend his Assistance in banking out this Inundation of Sound, which, if it finds a clear Passage, will not fail to overwhelm us in a Deluge of Folly and Absurdity.

—Mather Byles, "The Bombastic and Grubstreet Style," *American Magazine and Historical Chronicle* (1745).

Contents

Introduction: Christopher Lasch and the
Politics of the Plain Style
STEWART WEAVER   I

A Note on the Text   43

I   Elementary Principles of Literary Construction   45

II   Conventions Governing Punctuation,
       Capitalization, Typography, and Footnotes   55

III   Characteristics of Bad Writing   75

IV   Words Often Misused   93

V   Words Often Mispronounced   113

VI   Proofreaders' Marks   117

       Index   119

Introduction

Christopher Lasch and the Politics of the Plain Style

STEWART WEAVER

On January 31, 1983, the sixteen students in Christopher Lasch's graduate seminar on American social thought at the University of Rochester came to class expecting a discussion of Charlotte Perkins Gilman and the feminist contribution to American progressivism. Instead they got a quiz on the basic principles of English composition according to William Strunk and E. B. White. Lasch had evidently so despaired of his graduate students' writing that even at the risk of injuring their doctoral dignities he had given them all copies of Strunk and White's classic primer, *The Elements of Style*, and required them to read it from start to finish, along with George Orwell's well-known essay "Politics and the English Language." Whether he formally served notice of the impending quiz is unclear; the results, in any case, were sufficiently discouraging to lead

The author thanks Peter Agree, Celia Applegate, Casey Blake, Robert Westbrook, and Suzanne Wolk for comments on and corrections to an earlier draft of this introduction.

him to repeat the exercise on February 14, displacing (or at least delaying) this time a discussion of John Dewey, William James, and "the anti-philosophy of Pragmatism." When several students still misplaced the apostrophe in a plural possessive, misused *which* for *that* in a restrictive clause, omitted the hyphen in a compound adjective, and persisted in using *disinterested* as a synonym for *uninterested*, Lasch reluctantly concluded that even Strunk and White could not help them and began to compile his own list of common compositional errors, beginning with *likely* ("Not to be used as an adverb") and *different* ("Should be followed by *from*, not *than*").

On a different front, meanwhile, or rather on a different corner of his desk, Lasch was assembling the sentences, paragraphs, and chapters that were to appear in 1984 as *The Minimal Self*, the sequel volume, in effect, to the best-selling *Culture of Narcissism* (1979) and, with *Haven in a Heartless World* (1977), the third of his famous book-length inquiries into the making of the modern American self. That the author of some of the most intricate, original, and controversial books of their time should have been simultaneously occupied in compiling an English grammar seems unlikely, and for a while in fact it was altogether unknown. Intending nothing other than a short style sheet for his own classroom use—something many teachers provide—Lasch saw no need to announce its (not *it's*; see below, p. 102) existence to the world. But as he continued to work on it through 1983 and 1984, adding entries as they randomly came to mind, the sheet began to assume the proportions of a tract (not *track*; see below, p. 111), and Lasch began to wonder whether it might not be of more general, or at least departmental, interest. On assuming the chairmanship of the history department at Rochester in July 1985, he broached the thought to his colleagues. Finding them generally receptive, he set to work in earnest that summer, turning his catalogue of errors into a full-fledged writing guide, a lively, readable, in-house alternative to *The Elements of Style*.

In its earliest reproducible form, *Plain Style*, as Lasch called it, with a characteristically appreciative nod toward the Puritans, was essentially complete by October 1985 (the very month, as it oddly happened, of E. B. White's death). Lasch originally wanted to have it typeset and printed in pamphlet or handbook form as a university publication, but when this proved beyond the department's means—$1,700 for 1,000 copies was the given estimate— and when his editor at Norton evinced little commercial interest, he settled for tape-bound, 8½-by-11-inch typescript photocopies under an original pen and ink cover provided for the purpose by his daughter, Kate. He continued to work at it intermittently thereafter, tucking handwritten additions or revisions into his own copy as they occurred to him over the years (and as the computer revolution wreaked further havoc on the English language). But he never, so far as I know, prepared a second, revised typescript. For our students' use here in Rochester, we have been reproducing annually as needed the original typescript as Lasch left it in 1985.

The present, published edition of *Plain Style* is thus the first in its final form. More important, eight years after Christopher Lasch's impoverishingly early death in 1994, it at last makes generally available his least expected and least known but perhaps most serviceable work. As the teachers and students at the University of Rochester who have benefited from its succinct wisdom for years will testify, *Plain Style* is, in the first instance, an indispensable guide to writing. Shorter and more accessible (and more current) even than *The Elements of Style*, it is nevertheless a worthy successor, a witty and instructive introduction to the principles of effective composition. At the same time, however, it is a distinctive and revealing addition to the published work of an eminent American historian and social critic. Of course *Plain Style* never attains to the extended critical brilliance of *The Culture of Narcissism* or *The True and Only Heaven* (1991), Lasch's final, monumental indictment of the liberal ideology of progress. But it is, as I hope to make clear, consistently shot through with the same animating interests and concerns. No mere pedant's primer, *Plain Style* is itself something of an essay in cultural criticism, a political treatise even, by one for whom directness, clarity, and honesty of expression were, no less than for George Orwell, essential to the living spirit of democracy.

*   *   *

In light of his eventual stature as an American historian, we do well to recall at the outset that Christopher Lasch's earliest and in some ways most abiding ambition was to be, more generally, a *writer*. As the son of a reporter and editorialist at the *Chicago Sun-Times* and the *St. Louis Post-Dispatch*, Lasch grew up thinking of writing as part of the unremarkable daily business of life: a calling, but also a craft with a set of accepted conventions. His father gave him a primitive printing press when he was little, no more than nine or so. "I was always printing up newspapers and stuff," Lasch later recalled.[1] From long hours spent down at the *Sun-Times*, watching his father bang out editorials on a typewriter, Lasch got it into his head that that was how one wrote, quickly and directly on the typewriter. And though in later life he would often take to writing by pen on legal pads, shirt-cardboards, used envelopes, magazine tear-sheets, or whatever scrap of paper lay ready to hand, the typewriter remained for him the primary tool of the trade. Only at the very end of his life, and then only out of sheer physical necessity, did Lasch accommodate himself, reluctantly, to the computer. Writing for him was a tactile thing, a matter of paper and ink.

In 1947, at the encouragement of a memorable ninth-grade history teacher, Lasch first read Samuel Eliot Morison's and Henry Steele Commager's revered textbook, *The Growth of the American Republic*, but he had little thought as yet of becoming a historian (not *an* historian; see below, pp. 94–95) himself, and still less, presumably, of marrying Commager's daughter, Nell. What he really

---

1. Richard Wightman Fox, "An Interview with Christopher Lasch," *Intellectual History Newsletter* 16 (1994): 3.

wanted, like many an adolescent in thrall to Ernest Hemingway, was to be a novelist, an ambition he took with him to Harvard in 1950 only to discover that his roommate, John Updike, showed considerably more promise than he in this direction. He took a lot of creative writing courses anyway, and eventually produced the obligatory young man's coming-of-age novel (not *Bildungsroman*; see par. 17). But nothing ever came of it. Though he did not recognize it consciously at the time, Lasch was clearly casting about for alternative authorial forms when his tutor in the History Honors program, Donald Meyer, began to introduce him to books like David Riesman's *The Lonely Crowd* and Denis de Rougemont's *Love in the Western World*. Here was history in the pointed form of social criticism, a form somewhat akin, Lasch found, to his father's editorial writing, but much more deeply informed by the study of history, literature, philosophy, and the social sciences. Where his father had necessarily been concerned "with public policy, strictly speaking, or with day-to-day commentary on party politics or administrative detail," the social critic, Lasch found, tried to catch "the general drift of the times, to show how a particular incident or policy or a distinctive configuration of sentiments holds up a mirror to society, revealing patterns that otherwise might go undetected."[2] Unaware as yet that "the job of writing wasn't just to poke holes and raise stupid, often trivial objections," Lasch's first response to Meyer's assignments was instinctively negative.[3] But in time books like *The Lonely Crowd*, together with others of the high literary order of W. J. Cash's *Mind of the South*, J. A. Huizinga's *Waning of the Middle Ages*, and Richard Hofstadter's *American Political Tradition*, gave him his sense of what historical writing could be and suggested to him his calling. In the fall of 1954, quite at the last minute and against the advice of his tutor, who thought

2. Casey Blake and Christopher Phelps, "History as Social Criticism: Conversations with Christopher Lasch," *Journal of American History* 80 (1994): 1313.
3. Fox, "An Interview," 5.

he should go to Europe and bum around for a while, Lasch joined the doctoral program in history at Columbia University.

What a let-down. Fresh from the epiphanal experiences of Meyer's honors seminar, where the emphasis was on the heady exchange of ideas, Lasch now found himself in a setting where the emphasis was ruthlessly professional. Figures of enormous intellectual significance to him later were all on the scene: Lionel Trilling, C. Wright Mills, Richard Hofstadter, Reinhold Niebuhr. But Lasch was so busy writing historiographical summaries that he did not even attend their lectures, much less get to know them. "I didn't understand who Trilling was or who Niebuhr was or even who Hofstadter was in the wider intellectual community," he later lamented. "I didn't grasp the significance of that intellectual moment."[4] Instead, to a degree that may help account for the depth of his mature antipathy to the professional ethos, Lasch dutifully kept his head down and concentrated on learning American history and passing his oral qualifying examinations. Had Hofstadter been his adviser, it might have been different: here, after all, was someone who emphatically brought the past to bear on contemporary events. But Lasch had the idea that he wanted to study the New Deal, and this necessarily led him not to Hofstadter but to William Leuchtenburg, who placed a more traditional pedagogical emphasis on archival research. ("He thought that a source really wasn't very interesting if it was published," Lasch later and unfairly recalled.) Hofstadter did hire him one summer to write prefaces to some of the sections of a documentary anthology he was editing; his "ruthless but gentle criticism" of those efforts did much to cure Lasch of his would-be novelist's tendency to rely on flowery rhetoric to conceal uncertainty of argument.[5] But Leuchtenburg remained his adviser, even when his interests moved from the New Deal to the Progressive era. On leaving Columbia in 1957, and be-

4. Fox, "An Interview," 7.
5. Fox, "An Interview," 6, 8; Blake and Phelps, "Conversations," 1314–15.

tween his first teaching stints at Williams College and Roosevelt University, Lasch spent a good deal of time traipsing around the country from one archive to another, amassing data about American responses to the Russian Revolution.

The American Liberals and the Russian Revolution, the Columbia dissertation that in 1962 became Lasch's first book, clearly reflects his training under Leuchtenburg. It is a careful, original, archivally based account of the progressive response to Bolshevism. It is also, one hastens to add in this context, impressively written — vivid, clear, and altogether free of the ponderous pedantries that usually beset the academic monograph. And to a greater degree than Lasch himself recognized, the book quietly marks the start of his lifelong interrogation of the liberal idea of progress. But the presentist argument it makes about "the continuity between the liberalism of 1917 and that of 1962" was, as Lasch later conceded, "kind of trumped up after the fact," thanks more to a desperately belated reading of George Kennan than to Lasch's own dutiful research.[6] And the whole diplomatic context of the book, the thematic focus on the intersection of domestic opinion and foreign affairs, while it continued to define Lasch's own political being in the crisis-ridden years of the early Cold War, was not one that he was to develop much further as a historian and writer. The Lasch we recognize, the historian as social critic, the inspired plain stylist, and (not unrelatedly) the unflinching scourge of left and right alike, emerged only in 1965 with *The New Radicalism in America*.

For all its importance in establishing Lasch's reputation and announcing his presence as a public intellectual, *The New Radicalism* was, even to him, an unexpected, inadvertent, even accidental book. As Lasch later told it, his deepening antipathy to the Cold

6. Lasch, *The American Liberals and the Russian Revolution* (New York, 1962), vii; Fox, "An Interview," 8. For Lasch's later excursions into American diplomacy and the Cold War, see the essays reprinted in his *World of Nations: Reflections on American History, Politics, and Culture* (New York, 1973), chs. 6, 13, 14, 15.

War, together with his growing disenchantment, in the wake of the U-2 affair, with George Kennan, Walter Lippmann, and the whole school of liberal realism they represented, had led him in the early 1960s to start reading people like C. Wright Mills, Dwight Macdonald, William Appleman Williams, and finally "the intimidating figures who stood behind them: Karl Marx and the whole Marxist tradition."[7] Macdonald especially moved him to an interest in "the problem of intellectuals" in modern American life. His growing interest in psychoanalysis, meanwhile, led Lasch to think that people's personal lives "might be interesting from the point of view of intellectual [and] cultural history."[8] And finally his belated discovery of Richard Hofstadter suggested not only the possibility of productive reengagement with the progressive tradition but also a kind of writing, a compelling blend of analysis and narrative, of scholarship and critical artistry.

Beyond these various substantive and stylistic inclinations, however, Lasch seems to have given surprisingly little thought to what his book would be about. The rough idea, as he understood it by the spring of 1963, was "a study of certain intellectuals of the Progressive era that would somehow throw light on the problem of what an intellectual was at a time when this concept was just coming into use," but he cannot be said to have pursued this very systematically.[9] He chose his individual subjects almost at random off his bookshelves or out of his undergraduate lectures. Apart from a brief foray into the Jane Addams papers that yielded nothing of interest to him (and evidently put him off archives forever), he did little original research, relying instead on leavings from his dissertation and a few other aborted or abandoned projects. He wrote the book in great haste while on leave from teaching in England, hitting on his main argument ("that modern radicalism or liberal-

7. Blake and Phelps, "Conversations," 1315.
8. Fox, "An Interview," 8.
9. Fox, "An Interview," 8.

ism can best be understood as a phase of the social history of the intellectuals") only late in the day, appending it awkwardly onto what was by then essentially a completed collection of biographical essays.[10] He did not demonstrate conclusively the newness of the new radicalism, nor, as Robert Westbrook points out in a retrospective appreciation of the book, did he establish the historical context for the emergence of "the intellectual as a social type," as the introduction promised, preferring instead to deduce that context from a fairly hackneyed theory of mass society and what Westbrook calls lyrical reworkings of sociological clichés.[11]

But if the argument was weak and the structure "a bit wobbly," as Lasch later admitted, the varied content of *The New Radicalism* was more thoughtful, more rigorous, and simply more interesting than anything he had written before.[12] In the historical essay, it turned out, this aspiring young writer had found his natural form, and once having found it, he never gave it up. All his subsequent books, even those conceived as such, take the form of assembled essays on discrete but related subjects. And though the essays became more pointed and provocative over the years, they never again (until, arguably, *The True and Only Heaven*) achieved the splendidly leisured balance of historical research and reflection that marks *The New Radicalism.* "I think the most valuable thing about your book is the steady flow of marginal insight about the people you've chosen, the intellectual life as vocation, and the development of our culture," wrote Hofstadter encouragingly, and anyone reading the book now almost forty years later will find it impossible not to agree.[13] The portraits of Jane Addams, Randolph Bourne,

10. Lasch, *The New Radicalism in America, 1889–1963: The Intellectual as a Social Type* (New York, 1965), ix.
11. Robert Westbrook, "In Retrospect: Christopher Lasch, *The New Radicalism,* and the Vocation of Intellectuals," *Reviews in American History* 23 (1995):182.
12. Fox, "An Interview," 9.
13. Richard Hofstadter to Lasch, 27 September 1964 (Lasch Papers).

Mabel Dodge Luhan, Lincoln Colcord, Colonel House, and Lincoln Steffens remain "models of the biographer's art," writes Westbrook, "combining an acute sensitivity to the dynamics of the inner lives of some very complicated individuals with a novelist's eye for the telling detail."[14] The thematic chapters on feminism, social reform as social control, and the *New Republic*'s response to the First World War are equally deft and fully contoured excursions into the defining dilemmas of the progressive period. The final chapter on the "anti-intellectualism of the intellectuals," conceived in part as a deliberate provocation of Hofstadter, extended the meditation on the new radicalism breathlessly into the 1960s before ending "in a clatter of loud Wagnerian chords" with the seemingly improbable figure of Norman Mailer.[15] The musical metaphor (Lasch's own) is apt, for in addition to the novelist's eye for the telling detail, Lasch had the musician's ear for the felicitous sound: an essential element, in his mind, to good writing, as *Plain Style* with its recurrent emphasis on the importance of *listening* to the words makes clear.

Not that Lasch gave a lot of thought to the elements of style in these years. "I simply wrote in the only way I knew how to write, for maximum clarity and economy," he later claimed. But with *The New Radicalism* he was consciously distancing himself from the academic world and addressing himself to readers who were not necessarily historians. For one thing, he was chronically broke and eager to write in a way that paid. But he was also driven, he said, "by a vague feeling that if this business was worth doing"—writing, he meant—"it was worth doing because it enabled you to enter into a larger conversation, to become a citizen in the republic of letters." Here, again, the potent example of Hofstadter was crucial. So too was the whole political atmosphere of the late 1950s and early 1960s: "the widespread feeling of helplessness in the face of impersonal forces that rolled on relentlessly." Of course it was

14. Westbrook, "In Retrospect," 184.
15. Lasch to William Leuchtenburg (copy), 14 May 1964 (Lasch Papers).

just that "feeling of helplessness" that led some to become activists and organizers. "On me," Lasch said, its "effect was to make me redouble my efforts to write in such a way that somebody would hear it, so that it might have some influence, however small, on the course of events that otherwise just seemed inexorably to unfold."[16]

This humanist faith in the republic of letters seems almost quaint now, but in the politically fraught atmosphere of the 1960s it seemed, to many on the left anyway, a brazen betrayal of the "movement." Lasch's friend and fellow historian Staughton Lynd in particular worried that in choosing critically to reflect on Jane Addams, say, rather than simply celebrate her, Lasch was, in effect, selling out the cause and "questioning the validity of radical action by exploring its psychic origins." Lasch strongly disagreed. "I consider it my job to try to understand Jane Addams, not to dilate endlessly on the truth and beauty of her works," he wrote to Lynd. "But in any case understanding how such a woman came to spend her life the way she did does not necessarily detract from the validity of her works. Why should it?"[17] Essentially at issue here, as Westbrook has explained, were rival conceptions of the vocational responsibility of intellectuals. Against messianic activism on the one hand, and academic seclusion or conformity on the other, Lasch was upholding a paradoxical ideal of "detached engagement."[18] "I am not advocating a fashionable cult of 'alienation' and demanding symbolic gestures of withdrawal and rejection," he explained to Leuchtenburg. "I am only demanding what the new radicals promised but drew back from, trying to see middle-class society from the outside in, and then using this perspective to analyze, criticize, argue, persuade, in one's 'work' or in one's polemics, it makes no difference."[19] In later years, Lasch would exchange, indeed almost

16. Blake and Phelps, "Conversations," 1319–21.
17. Staughton Lynd, "Jane Addams and the Radical Impulse," *Commentary* (July 1961): 54; Lasch to Staughton Lynd (copy), 16 June 1964 (Lasch Papers).
18. Westbrook, "In Retrospect," 185–89.
19. Lasch to William Leuchtenburg (copy), 17 July 1965 (Lasch Papers).

invert this ideal of "detached engagement" in favor of Michael Walzer's notion of "connected" criticism. Rather than adopt the lofty, anthropological perspective of the outcast or stranger, connected critics, as he understood it, "stand within the society under criticism. Their position is one of provisional loyalty. They hold a society up to its own highest standards, appeal to its own traditions in order to show how far its practice falls sort of its principles." The perfect perspective, in other words, turned out to be rather more from the inside out than the outside in. But to the end Lasch maintained that critical detachment—"that is, the willingness to submit one's own ideas, one's own positions to the same standards, to the same skepticism that one applies to others"—was essential to good historical writing and the political purpose that it served.[20] He had a remarkably sustained abhorrence for the party line.

After finishing *The New Radicalism in America*, Lasch had hoped to return to a book he had long been contemplating "on women or the family or marriage or whatever it was." But he was more and more distracted by politics—"who wasn't in the late 1960s"—and more and more doubtful of his ability to write "a real book."[21] Meanwhile, on the strength of the response to *The New Radicalism*, Lasch found himself in regular demand as an occasional reviewer and essayist, and it was in this vein, especially by way of his robust essays in the *New York Review of Books*, that he first entered public consciousness. "His ken astonished," Jean Elshtain recalls of her own discovery of Lasch. "He wrote with equal facility and discernment about American foreign policy, the twists and turns of the New Left, the vagaries of American history generally, the family, psychoanalysis, education, the emerging therapeutic mentality, popular culture."[22] More generally, at a time

20. Blake and Phelps, "Conversations," 1329. For Michael Walzer's own discussion of connected criticism, see his *Company of Critics* (New York, 1988).
21. Fox, "An Interview," 10.
22. Jean Bethke Elshtain, "Christopher Lasch, American," *Tikkun* 9, 3 (1994): 57.

of great political trauma—we are talking about the late 1960s and early 1970s now—Lasch preserved a rare space for reasoned dissent against the forces of bureaucratic and technological regimentation on the one hand, and nihilist revolt on the other. His subjects were ephemeral, some of them, and in their collected forms as *The Agony of the American Left* (1969) and *The World of Nations* (1973), Lasch's *New York Review* essays have worn unevenly; they seldom figure in retrospective reconstructions of his career. But they were vital at the time both for their strong application of historical understanding to contemporary concerns and for their practical demonstration of that paradoxical stance of "detached engagement" that *The New Radicalism* had more dimly imagined.

Furthermore (and more to the present purpose), it is to these essays of the late 1960s that we can trace the concern with the politics of language that would inform the writing of *Plain Style* almost twenty years later. These were, after all, the climactic years of the American "intervention" in Vietnam. Political circumstances demanded of those in power a defense of the indefensible by way of ever more euphemism, jargon, evasion, and downright lying. "Defenceless villages are bombarded from the air, the inhabitants driven out into the countryside, the cattle machine-gunned, the huts set on fire with incendiary bullets: this is called *pacification*. Millions of peasants are robbed of their farms and sent trudging along the roads with no more than they can carry: this is called *transfer of population* or *rectification of frontiers*."[23] The same rhetorical tendency that George Orwell thus indicted in 1946, in the context of the death throes of European colonialism and the Russian deportations, reached a whole new standard of perfection in the age of Vietnam, and Lasch responded like Orwell before him, relentlessly exposing the monstrous and contemptible truths that lay behind the evasive jargon of White House, State Department, and

23. George Orwell, "Politics and the English Language," repr. in *The Collected Essays, Journalism and Letters of George Orwell* (New York, 1968), 4: 136.

Pentagon. He meted out the same deflating treatment to Washington's domestic policy elite, those self-styled "future-planners" who believed that "social accounting" would solve all of America's social "problems."[24]

Of course honesty and clarity of language suffered not only at the hands of governing elites during the Vietnam War. Anti-war activists and radical reformers had their own favorite forms of doublespeak, and if Lasch reserved most of his ire for these, it was only because here he had hoped for something better. As one who, despite his misgivings about activism, had stood up to confront the State Department's "truth squad" when it rolled into Iowa City (where Lasch was teaching at the time) "with orders to correct the dangerous errors spread by academic opponents of the war," he had taken heart, he later recalled, "from the growing opposition to the war, from the formation of a new left, and from the student movement's attempt to explain the connection between the war and the bureaucratization of academic life."[25] But the more the new left degenerated into revolutionary histrionics, the more obsessed it became with ideological purity and the sentimentalization of outcast groups, the less it appealed to one of Lasch's independent disposition. As early as 1965, in fact, Lasch had already been disturbed by the new left's tendency to forsake "the language of criticism, the Western tradition of rational discourse for the obscurantist jargon of the 'movement.' "[26] By 1969, with the splintering of the SDS, the dispersal of the antiwar movement, and the eclipse of the forces of respectable dissent by such "clownish media freaks" as Jerry Rubin and Abbie Hoffman, his disillusion was more or less complete. In

24. Lasch, "The Cultural Cold War," in *The Agony of the American Left* (New York, 1969), 114. For Lasch on Vietnam, see "The Foreign Policy Elite and the War in Vietnam," in *The World of Nations*, 232–49. For his dread of the much overused and misused word "problem," see below, p. 108.
25. Lasch, *The True and Only Heaven: Progress and Its Critics* (New York, 1991), 27.
26. Lasch to William Leuchtenburg (copy), 17 July 1965 (Lasch Papers).

momentary despair of American politics and the whole promise of American life, he now immersed himself in European social theory, especially the work of the Frankfurt school, whose synthesis of Marx and Freud seemed to him to provide Marxism for the first time with a "serious theory of culture," and the tradition of English Marxism, which, as articulated by Raymond Williams and E. P. Thompson, "showed how Marxism could absorb the insights of cultural conservatives and provide a sympathetic account, not just of the economic hardships imposed by capitalism, but of the way in which capitalism thwarted the need for joy in work, stable connections, family life, a sense of place, and a sense of historical continuity."[27]

The first fruit of Lasch's own distinctive cross-breeding of American history and European social theory, *Haven in a Heartless World: The Family Besieged*, appeared after long gestation in 1977. Originally conceived as the theoretical introduction to a longer history of women and the family that in the end he would never complete, *Haven* was, he later recalled, the most difficult of all his books to write. And no wonder. He was now not merely performing an extremely delicate political balancing act not so much between left and right as above and beyond them — entering into what British historians would recognize as his "Tory Radical" phase. He was also trying to bring the requirements of the plain style — clarity, economy, accessibility — to bear on an intricate, highly technical, and theoretically challenging subject. The level of response in simple terms of copies sold, reviewed, and read might be reckoned a measure of great success: *Haven* made Lasch almost a household name. But it also generated more heat than light (as Lasch himself conceded) and was the first (though not the last) of his books to be widely misunderstood. In his preface to the 1979 paperback edition, Lasch tried to turn this into a political point of pride. Only unreconstructed ideologues of left and right had misunderstood him,

27. Lasch, *The True and Only Heaven*, 27–29.

he said. Only to those for whom politics consisted of "ready-made answers and automatic loyalties" had *Haven* presented itself as a "difficult," "obscure," and "recondite" book.[28] Point taken. But it is undeniable that as he moved out of cultural history into sociology by way of Marx and Freud, Lasch was becoming more difficult to read, even for the open minded, and the tone of the 1979 preface suggests both defensiveness and ambivalence on this score.

Little did he know then, of course, that, difficult or not, he was on the verge of reaching more readers than he had ever hoped for or even really wanted. Distracted once again from his history of women and whatever, Lasch had since the appearance of *Haven* been writing a number of essays on closely related but more explicitly psychoanalytical themes: the awareness movement, the therapeutic sensibility, sex war, the family, the new illiteracy, paternalism, the new narcissism. No sooner had *Haven* appeared, in fact, than he thought he might have the stuff of a good book here under the organizing theme of "the narcissistic personality of our time." But his editor at Knopf, unchagrined it seems by the egregious mistake of having already passed on *Haven* (which came out from Basic Books), passed on this manuscript too, saying "all this is just one more book of essays."[29] Lasch knew this was wrong: he had gone to much more trouble than he had with either *The Agony of the American Left* or *The World of Nations* to produce an integrated book with one coherent argument. And the strength of the response to *Haven*, however muddled it had been, confirmed for him that he was on to something potentially big. Even so, nothing had prepared him, intellectually or emotionally, for the response that met *The Culture of Narcissism* when it appeared under the Norton imprint in

28. Lasch, *Haven in a Heartless World: The Family Besieged*, paperback ed. (New York, 1979), xiii. The nearest thing we will ever have to Lasch's long-projected book on women and the family is *Women and the Common Life: Love, Marriage, and Feminism* (New York, 1997), a posthumous collection of essays edited by his daughter, Elisabeth Lasch-Quinn.
29. Fox, "An Interview," 11.

early 1979. It was vast, vigorous, and instantaneous. Had he known, Lasch later said, that the book was going to end up on the *New York Times* best-seller list, he would have written it somewhat differently. After all, some of it is fairly technical. The psychoanalytic chapters especially come out of "a distinctive scholarly tradition," Lasch said, "and for a more popular book it would have been a good idea to explain all of that, to situate that tradition, to argue why that tradition seemed to provide a useful perspective on our society."[30] As one who struggled through the book at age twenty-one in some perplexity as to what all the fuss was about, I'm inclined to agree here: some basic orientation would have helped. But it also, I see now, would have compromised the intellectual and stylistic integrity of a book that without any pretension, condescension, or fanfare gives the general reader the benefit of the doubt and asks him or her to enter with the author into rich cultural complexities. To write *plainly*, after all, is emphatically not to write *simply*, let alone *simplemindedly*, as Lasch more than anyone knew. "In *The Culture of Narcissism* I was trying to do the same thing I've always tried to do," he later, more confidently, recalled, "which is to write as lucidly as possible for an audience that cannot be presumed to know all the ins and outs of whatever body of scholarship may underlie the argument I'm trying to make, but that is capable of understanding them once they are explained in a fairly clear fashion."[31]

And once they are laid out, he might have added, on a fairly clear page. For the warrant of the plain style did not end with the choice and arrangement of the words. For Lasch, an accomplished amateur bookbinder and printer, a craftsman in the truest, traditional sense, it extended to the mechanical matters of paper, margins, and ink. "He always took special interest in style and production and in all the visible and tactile aspects of his books," Jeannette Hopkins, who edited two of them for Norton, recalls. Indeed, the

30. Fox, "An Interview," 11–12.
31. Fox, "An Interview," 12.

indifference of Basic Books to his views in these matters when it came to *Haven* had much to do with his determination to take *Narcissism* elsewhere, and once at Norton he took particular, even contractual care to get what he wanted, namely, a "well-designed, good-looking" book, uniform in appearance with the three that had been published by Knopf. He preferred a 5½ x 8¼ trim to the more conventional 6 x 9, he explained, "because the page contains a more manageable number of words and a shorter line of type, the book is lighter and easier to hold, and the whole object gener-ally has more satisfying proportions, at least where the text runs to medium length (say, 90,000 to 150,000 words) and therefore takes on a spindly, emaciated appearance when issued in the larger for-mat." He liked sewn not glued bindings—he did not get one, not this time—good paper ("which takes ink—a strange substance that is still actually used by many readers, including myself"), rough and not clean cut pages, colored end-papers, and type large enough to read without a magnifying glass. Among typefaces he preferred Janson—a sturdy, seventeenth-century Dutch type, appropriately enough—but would accept any of those "in common use today, such as Caledonia, Electra, Times Roman, Granjon [the typeface of his Knopf books], or Primer." He wanted his quotations run-in, not set off, regardless of their length. As *Plain Style* would empha-size, he favored sparing use of capital letters: president, constitu-tion, congressional, old left, new left, narcissism. And he insisted on reserving the honorific "Dr." for those with a medical degree—physicians, psychiatrists, *at least* psychoanalysts, but emphatically *not* professors. "All of these seem like fussy, even obsessive, de-tails," Hopkins further recalls, "*not one* of them critical, alone, but together they added up to something big": a book both clearly and provocatively written *and* elegantly and artfully arrayed, and there-fore all the more satisfying to have, to hold, to read, and to ponder.[32]

32. For this paragraph, I have drawn on the typescript of a forthcoming book on authors and editors by Jeannette Hopkins, editor of *The Culture of Narcis-*

The Culture of Narcissism, a national best-seller that hit the pages of *Time* and *Newsweek*, became a mass-market paperback, and ended in an invitation to the White House (where it was said to have informed Jimmy Carter's famous "national malaise" speech of July 1979), was in certain obvious respects a hard act to follow. Despite his growing public reputation as a cantankerous curmudgeon, a killjoy full of bile and spleen, Lasch, as anyone who ever met him will recall, was a surpassingly quiet, gentle, modest, and even-tempered man. He was clearly uncomfortable with the celebrity status he had suddenly acquired and anxious somehow to deflect it without giving up his intellectual prominence. At the same time, he felt intellectually and vocationally at sea, quite unsure, for the first time in years, of where as a writer he was going. With *Haven* and *Narcissism*, he said, he had freed himself from the professionalism he had learned at Columbia and no longer felt under any obligation to impress a body of historians. Yet he was sick of psychoanalysis, sick of the Frankfurt school, sick of the whole Freudian-Marxist turn his work had taken, and eager to return to a more historical and vernacular idiom. In *The Minimal Self*, the book based upon his reluctant re-immersion in psychoanalysis for the purposes of the 1981 Freud Lectures at University College, London, one begins to discern an unfamiliar openness to religion, to the Judeo-Christian tradition of moral prophecy. In his several contributions to *democracy*, Sheldon Wolin's short-lived attempt to join academic scholarship and social criticism in the early 1980s, one senses a yearning for "an indigenous American tradition of speculation and action," a growing identification with the common sense and common decency of middle America, and, portentously, an ever-sharpening skepticism toward any philosophy or ideology of progress. But where precisely these disparate lines of thought were tending was as yet unclear

---

sism and *The True and Only Heaven*, and on several Lasch letters and Norton memoranda now in her archive at the Vassar College Library. My thanks to Ms. Hopkins for her permission to quote this material.

when *The Minimal Self* appeared with a more or less resounding thud in 1984. Meanwhile, Lasch had classes to teach, lectures to give, and papers, papers, always more papers to grade.[33]

*   *   *

"I am grading papers with the usual sense of futility," wrote Lasch to his father in May 1985 (not May *of* 1985; see below, par. 26). "I keep simplifying my course in 20th century American history, but the students keep getting dumber faster than I can simplify it. Every year the illiteracy gets worse."[34] And every year it surely weighed more heavily on Lasch's mind. The general debasement of political language had long been a theme of his review essays, as we have seen. Since the early 1970s at least, he had been objecting in passing to the popular (and inaccurate) use of such crucial terms to him as "behavior," "revolution," "tradition," "problem," and "nostalgia." But only with *The Culture of Narcissism* do we get a full-blown lament over "the spread of stupefaction" and "the new illiteracy." Resisting the easy temptation to blame the teachers, the schools, or (even more commonly) the students, Lasch there pointed to sweeping historical changes in the home and workplace that underlay the deterioration of education and the growing inability of American citizens "to use language with ease and precision, to recall the basic facts of their country's history, to make logical deductions, to understand any but the most rudimentary written texts, or even to grasp their constitutional rights."[35] The further inability of most people to grasp the argument of *The Culture of Narcissism*, their tendency in particular to misread it as simply an indignant outcry against hedonism, naturally discouraged him still more. But it was the grading, the regular, relent-

33. Fox, "An Interview," 12–13; Blake and Phelps, "Conversations," 1328, 1332.
34. Lasch to Robert N. Lasch, 6 May 1985 (Lasch Papers).
35. Lasch, *The Culture of Narcissism*, 128.

less, terribly important but increasingly frustrating work of student grading that finally pushed him over the edge and drove him to write *Plain Style*. To single out one student paper, even pseudonymously, is unfair; to violate Lasch's own prohibition on lengthy quotation perhaps unforgivable. But only in its entirety will this written comment, Lasch's response to a (let's hope) undergraduate paper on American pragmatism, convey the scale of the pedagogical challenge he faced and the serious (and occasionally sarcastic) spirit in which he met it:

> Daniel—
>
> It just isn't possible to follow this paper. You seem to be talking about something important, but the words go by in a blur. They seem to refer to things one has heard of, but they don't actually make any statement about them. Consider a few examples. "James was more the philosopher in the sense that he did not form any direct modes of institution." This sentence is so obscure that I can't even begin to explain what's wrong with it. The phrase "direct modes of institution" simply doesn't make any sense. But the main trouble is that it isn't clear what "more" refers to. James more than Dewey and Holmes?
>
> Another example. "Although these movements are by no means identical, they shared the arrival of a faith which relied upon a unique orientation of how they viewed man's essance [sic] . . ." Here we get off to a pretty good start, but the sentence then dissolves in confusion. Pragmatism, you say, has something in common with Marxism and existentialism—namely, the "arrival" of a faith. "Arrival" is terribly confusing here; but what follows is even worse. It just doesn't say anything. It seems to say something; that is, the medium is words; but the words aren't arranged in any grammatical or conceptual order. Their arrangement seems completely arbitrary. The words would make as much sense

if we rearranged them arbitrarily and said that pragmatism shared with Marxism and existentialism a faith "which relied upon a viewed unique man's orientation of essence."

A third example, more forbidding still. "The culture the progressive era followed was different, the claim is that both the general culture and academic philosophy from the last quarter of the nineteenth century to the first quarter of the twentieth century, are offspring of a culture in which philosophy constituted a central form of social activity in which its role and function was very unlike the progressive culture which found itself subjected to modernization via the industrial revolution." The sentence resists all attempts to translate it into English. It is grammatically incoherent in all its parts. Do you know what you meant to say? It's like reading a foreign language. In most examples of bad writing in student papers, I can puzzle out the thought and suggest better ways of expressing it. Here I am completely baffled—not just by this particular sentence but by practically every other sentence in your paper. The grade [C] reflects my belief that you've done a good deal of reading, struggled to understand it, and tackled a very hard subject, furthermore. Still, it is a generous grade. In a way, there's no basis for a grade at all, since I have no idea what you're trying to say. It's as if words had taken flight into an airy realm of their own where they no longer refer recognizably to things or ideas but just kind of mix and mingle and rub shoulders with each other in a friendly kind of just us folks and abstract terribly with jargon and heavy academic, to which makes no difference how you arrange, to read backwards and if you read from the middle it doesn't seem to matter.

A lot of this, I think, has to do with a certain failure to attend to words when used by others. Maybe this is a generational thing; maybe (as some have suggested) it is a function of too much TV; yours, in any case, is an extreme example of what may be a general tendency to respond to words not on the level of their sense but on a more emotional level, not as aids to communication but as signals indicating a *desire* to communicate, as when people follow every sentence with "You know?" or "'Kay?" The words in this paper indicate in a vague way that the subject is philosophy, that philosophy is going to be considered in an academic way, that the writer has done a lot of reading in heavy and dull books. This is the real content of the paper, as far as I can make out. The words are meant to convey a general impression of hard intellectual labor. But what if you were asking directions to the airport and had only ten minutes to catch your plane? Or worse, what if you were giving directions to someone whose life might depend on getting there in time? Would you use such language as this?

As I was saying, the trouble may begin in the way words are listened to in the first place—a kind of systematic in-attention, encouraged, perhaps, by the habitual inattention with which people watch television. (Note that they don't listen to it, or see it; they merely *watch* it—a succession of flickering images signifying nothing.) A single example will make my point, I hope. You have managed to write a whole paper about American pragmatism (or rather, about writing a paper about pragmatism) and to refer to one of its leading exponents, throughout, as "Pierre." How is it possible to confuse "Peirce" with "Pierre," unless one's mind is simply somewhere else? We're not talking about some obscure no-body, we're talking about the founder of the movement the paper is supposed to be all about. *Pierre*??????

Well . . . an extreme case, perhaps, but one that, besides show-ing the remarkable time and care that Lasch took with his students' papers, alerts us to all the compositional tendencies and habits of mind that he was to deplore at greater length in *Plain Style*: gram-

matical incoherence, academic ponderousness, systematic inattentiveness, verbal deafness, and a general failure to respond to words
on the level of their sense and meaning. The comment is undated.
Preserved as it is, however, among the early working drafts of *Plain
Style*, it must be contemporary with them and represent something
like a formative fragment. In this one hapless paper on American
pragmatism, we have, I think, the final provocation.

The formal occasion, though, of Lasch's decision to write
Plain Style was his assumption of the chairmanship of the history
department in July 1985. By then he had been at the University
of Rochester for fifteen years, having left Northwestern in 1970
in order to join Eugene Genovese (whose work on the history of
American slavery he much admired) in shaping a department that
would be "fairly explicitly committed to the enterprise of historically informed social criticism and at the same time not committed
to any specific form of it."[36] Alas, not all his new colleagues shared
this vision, and even those who did—Genovese among them—
turned out to be at least as committed to academic and political
in-fighting. Lasch arrived to a department both deeply and dys-
functionally divided. So he bided his time, wrote his books, helped
raise his children, and yes, tended his own garden—he was an ex-
pert gardener—while the spirit of the 1970s played itself out in
parody around him.

By 1985, finally, things in the history department and in the
university generally were, Lasch thought, looking up. Genovese,
his divisive energies momentarily spent, had been cast out into an
extra-departmental wilderness before leaving Rochester altogether
in 1986. The university had a new, dynamic, and philosophically
inclined president named Dennis O'Brien, who actually had the
faculty "talking about education" and of whom Lasch, therefore, initially entertained high hopes.[37] O'Brien's inaugural idea

36. Christopher Phelps interview with Lasch, 23 July 1993 (unpublished and
unabridged typescript in author's possession).
37. Lasch to Richard Fox, 30 April, 1985 (Lasch Papers).

of changing the name of the university to reflect its new national aspirations foundered on the shoals of local resistance, but it did bring the place much-needed (if rather ironic) publicity. It was in this generally rejuvenative atmosphere that Lasch took on the chairmanship in 1985, in hopes not only of "arresting the department's gradual decline," as he put it to Edward Berenson, a former student, but also of creating the kind of lively, collaborative intellectual community that he thought he was joining in 1970.[38] As a condition of his office, he secured several new faculty appointments in American and European history: the department's first appointments in these fields in ten years. With the encouragement (and financial sponsorship) of the new administration, he envisioned a series of high-profile, interdisciplinary seminars on "the current state of knowledge in the humanities and social sciences to counter the trend toward narrowly empirical scholarship inaccessible to a broader public and to rehabilitate the idea of public philosophy."[39] He hoped the department might undertake a series of published pamphlets—the "Yellowjacket Series" he called it, after the university's improbable mascot—to fill what he saw as the yawning gap between the historical monograph and the text book. And, in a letter to his son at least, he imagined an "annual newsletter containing reviews of recent work, historiographical articles, etc., written entirely by students, or at least principally by students," the idea being to train them in the work of summary, exposition, and critical assessment: in sum, in "the historiographical arts."[40]

38. Lasch to Edward Berenson, 24 June 1985 (Lasch Papers).
39. Lasch to Robert N. Lasch, 6 May 1985 (Lasch Papers).
40. Coming from Lasch, this call to the work of summary and exposition seems strangely professional—just the kind of thing he had unhappily endured at Columbia and then forsworn. But as the paradoxical phrase "historiographical arts" suggests, he had something different and nobler in mind. His hope, as he explained it to Richard Fox, was for the department "to play some part in a critical reevaluation of the state of the historical discipline, thereby making some modest contribution to the development of a more vocational (as opposed to careerist) definition of professionalism—on which the prospects

Plain Style thus emerged in 1985 as part of a much larger, intellectually elaborate local project. In published isolation, some years after the fact, it may look like a generic primer, an all-purpose guide, as the subtitle said, to written English. And so on one level it was meant to be and is. But in Lasch's mind it was also a preliminary, pedagogical step toward a particular vision of a history department, and as such it had to be distinctive. Not that it had to address itself to the particular compositional needs of historians; these Lasch would have denied or at least disowned as pseudoprofessional and pretentiously academic. But it had to be more historically minded than, say, *The Elements of Style*, more evocative somehow of Anglo-American literary traditions, and more inclined to encourage not just the kind of writing, but the kind of thinking about the past that Lasch approved and that lent itself to "the historiographical arts" as he understood them.

Consider in this light the title, *Plain Style*, which immediately distinguishes Lasch's guide from more practically minded rivals like Sheridan Baker's *The Practical Stylist* or William Zinsser's *On Writing Well*. Even Strunk and White, for whom plainness was, along with simplicity, orderliness, and sincerity, one of the four cardinal compositional virtues, refrained from giving it this exclusive, titular emphasis. For "plain" is not as . . . well . . . plain a word as it appears. Easily enough defined (by the *American Heritage Dictionary*) to mean open, clear, evident, apparent, straightforward, frank, or candid, "plain" has a number of secondary meanings that in both English and American ears soon start to resonate more pointedly and politically. Common, average, ordinary, unaffected, honest, pure, uncorrupted: "plain" in these senses shades into the language of populism. The plain style is in fact a populist style; its masters historically are Swift, Cobbett, Mencken, Chesterton, and, supremely, Orwell, who more than Strunk or White or Baker

for democracy may now largely depend." Lasch to Chris Lasch, 23 July 1985; Lasch to Richard Fox, 30 April 1985 (Lasch Papers).

or Zinsser or any other semantic authority was the abiding spirit behind Lasch's *Plain Style*. For Orwell appreciated the political stakes involved; he knew that the fight against bad English was no frivolous matter of received pronunciation or standard usage, but "a necessary step towards political regeneration," as he put it in "Politics and the English Language." Lasch drove the point home in the answer key to his first writing quiz. "Language is a political question, according to Orwell," he explained to his students, "because the corruption of language originates in a political condition, the need to defend policies that would arouse opposition if they were clearly understood." Thus, against the pretentious (*phenomenon, element, objective*), trite (*epic, epoch-making, age-old*), archaic (*realm, throne, banner, clarion*), and Latinate (*expedite, ameliorate, extraneous, deracinated*) diction favored by those in power on the left or the right, Orwell encouraged a simple, sturdy, plain, Saxon style—"I watched a man hanged once"—the whole purpose of which was to arouse the political indignation of ordinary people. This, by 1985, was Lasch's purpose too. In despair now of the capacity of either Freudian or Marxist language actually to move people's minds, or even to convey clearly what he thought about things, he embraced the plain style as a necessary complement to his emerging populism, to his new-found Orwellian regard for the common sense and decency of plain folk.[41]

Stronger still than *Plain Style*'s populist overtones, though, are its Puritan ones. Plainness is historically a protestant virtue. It suggests austerity, humility, acceptance, dependence, patience, and gratitude: all qualities of increasing significance to Lasch's world view as he abandoned the Freudian idiom, or rather assimilated it to a much older tradition of moral discourse. One could indulge a whole essay at this point on Lasch's evolving attitude toward religion. A militant secularist by inheritance, he had arrived by the end

41. See George Orwell, "Politics and the English Language," 128, 131; Lasch, "Answers to Quiz," 31 January 1983 (Lasch Papers).

of his life at what he described as an "openness" to religion, a "willingness to listen," a reluctance "to write off this whole realm of experience as if it didn't matter." [42] That he was on the road to Rome at the time of his death, as some have contrived to imagine, is surely mistaken: of the nineteenth century's two great anti-modernists, Thomas Carlyle, loomed considerably larger for him than John Henry Newman; austerity, not asceticism was his ideal. [43] But in his growing recognition of the inescapable limits on human power, in his insistence on the sinfulness of our rebellion against those limits, in his emphasis on the redemptive value of work, "which at once signifies man's submission to necessity and enables him to transcend it," one rightly perceives as in Carlyle before him a real indebtedness to the Calvinist tradition of Christian prophecy. [44] If not precisely religious, Lasch was "religiously musical," as his friend Robert Coles observed; his late work may reasonably be construed as "an attempt to find and to secure secular sources that would offer occasion for the stories of human sin and redemption, the coming to grips with evil in oneself and the world generally, the possibilities of grace and awe found in religion or, to be more precise, in the Christian narrative." [45]

Plain Style discloses its Puritan inspiration at several points. The title and leading epigraph come from William Bradford's *History of Plymouth Plantation* (c. 1650), the original chronicle of the Pilgrim settlement by its second and longest-serving governor. The supporting epigraphs come from William Ames (1576-1633), a seventeenth-century English Puritan divine and controversialist whose views on universal redemption and election won him an influential following in the Low Countries, and Mather Byles (1706-88), an American Congregational clergyman and poet known for

42. Fox, "An Interview," 13.
43. Cf. Dale Vree, "Christopher Lasch: A Memoir," *New Oxford Review* (April 1994), 2–5.
44. Lasch, *The True and Only Heaven*, 240.
45. Elshtain, "Christopher Lasch, American," 57–58.

his scholarly sermons and ready wit and descended, on his mother's side, from John Cotton and Richard Mather. Lasch's entry on *principal* and *principle* subtly engages William Ellery Channing's distinctly un-Calvinist view "that God arranges things for the happiness and convenience of human beings" (see below, p. 107), and here and there we get a passing reference to Jonathan Edwards (1703–58), another ardent, Puritan divine, whose renunciationist conception of "true virtue" was to figure centrally in *The True and Only Heaven*. But then we get passing references to Steve Garvey and Antonio Gramsci too. The Puritan emphasis of *Plain Style* lies less in its occasional epigraphs and illustrative allusions than in its sustained thematic insistence on stylistic austerity and straightforward, unadorned devotion to "the commonplace facts of everyday life." What had been, in Strunk and White, a practical rule of thumb—"Omit needless words"—becomes in Lasch something more like a moral law.

In many respects, in scale and in format, *Plain Style* follows *The Elements of Style* closely. Lasch loved and admired "the little book," as William Strunk had called it long before E. B. White came along and brought it to the notice of the world. It had long been a staple of his teaching. By 1985, however, he found that it assumed more grammatical knowledge than most students had and that it did not deal with many mistakes that had become commonplace since White's published revision of 1957. So he set out on something like his own revision, beginning, as Strunk had done, with some elementary rules of punctuation and usage. It was only when his colleague MacGregor Knox pointed out that even those students who could write a passable sentence had trouble composing an essay (or even a paragraph) that he appended the present opening chapter on the "elementary principles of literary construction."[46] The very phrase recalls Strunk and White's "elementary

46. An accomplished plain stylist himself, Knox also made a number of smaller suggestions for inclusion in Lasch's guide, as did Sanford Elwitt, another col-

principles of composition," the title to their chapter 2. But where Strunk had proceeded in the form of sharp rules and commands— "Use the active voice," "Put statements in a positive form," "Omit needless words," "Keep related words together"—Lasch proceeded in the subtler form of a short, exemplary essay. *Two* exemplary essays, in fact: his own, emphasizing the need in every composition for a discernible beginning, middle, and end, and one by Randolph Bourne that to his mind showed better than any list of rules how a fairly complex argument could be contained in a small compass, "without any ostentatious display of erudition, without the usual spiteful attacks on the work of other authorities in the field, without elaborate preliminaries or tedious summations, and without the crab-like sideways motion and backtracking that so often characterize the work of inexperienced [and experienced, alas] writers," (below, p. 53).

Lasch's choice of Randolph Bourne (1886–1918) to demonstrate the basic elements of prose composition was, needless to say, not arbitrary. Not only was Bourne a recognized master of the short essay; he was one of Lasch's favorite thinkers, an alter ego even, from *The New Radicalism in America*, where he stands out as one of the few progressive intellectuals to resist the tawdry temptations of "the movement" in favor of a richer conception of politics as a "means to life," to *The True and Only Heaven*, where he figures alongside Thorstein Veblen, John Dewey, Lewis Mumford, Van Wyck Brooks, and Waldo Frank as a rare American champion of participatory as opposed to distributive democracy. Against those for whom universal abundance, affluence, and leisure held out the best hope of cultural democracy, Bourne, like Lasch after him, defended the older, simpler ideal of competence, sufficiency, and labor. But his particular concern, as a writer and

---

league in European history. In fact, although Lasch was the sole author, *Plain Style* was, in spirit at least, a collaborative project. Across all personal and political divides, it reflected a shared departmental commitment to good writing.

critic, was American education, and thus his usefulness to Lasch's present purpose. The essay is about the "baffling resistance of the undergraduate mind." It is an effort to account for why American students, for all their diligent attention to fact and detail, seem impervious to points of view or interpretations, seem to lack philosophy, in a word, and pass out of college without anything like the European's intellectual impress. Seventy years later—Bourne's essay first ran in the *New Republic* in 1915—these questions were still much on Lasch's mind, and like Bourne's his inclination was to blame not the students but the university for its capitulation to the "vague moral optimism" and the "sporting philosophy" of middle America. All this may seem far afield from matters of style and grammar. But again, *Plain Style* must be understood as part of a larger institutional project, and Lasch began it by holding out a vision of the ultimate end in view: a college life "less like that of an undergraduate country club," as Bourne put it, "and more of an intellectual workshop where men and women in the fire of their youth, with conflicts and idealism, questions and ambitions and desire for expression, come to serve an apprenticeship under the masters of the time."

Lasch's accompanying commentary on Bourne's essay is a short exercise in summary exposition, one of "the historiographical arts" he was especially keen to teach. Part II then introduces the more mundane matters of punctuation, typography, and notation. But even here Lasch manages to suggest larger cultural themes and lend *Plain Style* something of his own critical personality. In the entry on "breathing spaces," for instance, he deplores the growing divide between written and spoken English and its bad effects, as he saw it, on literary style. In general, Puritan that he was, Lasch approved the move away from the ornate punctuation, the dashes, italics, and "superabundance of typographical symbols of all sorts that characterized written English in the eighteenth and early nineteenth centuries." Gratuitous use of quotation marks, whether to signify irony or sarcasm or "to establish a certain lofty distance from the commonplace facts of everyday life," he especially deplored. But he cherished the comma, which he found essential to preserving the rhythms of spoken language on the printed page. Journalists, scholars, ad writers, copy editors, English composition teachers, . . . even the eminent authority of the *Chicago Manual of Style* might find it a relic, a rude intrusion on our streamlined modern style. But Lasch defended the comma on behalf of the plain reader, for whom writing was merely vicarious speech. Here a point of grammar becomes a folk cause, one small expression of a kind of syntactical populism.

Once we are alert to it, we can detect Lasch's distinctive voice in even the most innocuous of these opening entries. Note how the straightforward recommendation against using contractions somehow evolves, in paragraph 10, into a pointed attack on the "therapeutic idiom of jaded urban sophistication." Following Orwell, Lasch discourages the use of foreign words and phrases as pretentious and showy. He forbids the new, two-letter state abbreviations—MA, MS—as "bureaucratic innovations designed to surround the postal service with an illusory air of efficiency." "The old abbreviations—Mass., Miss.—are sanctified by custom," he says, and therefore much to be preferred (par. 22). Acronyms similarly fall under Lasch's general prohibition on bureaucratic speech. "The widespread use of initials tends either to lend suspect purposes a spurious air of importance and dignity," he notes, or "to make remote bureaucratic agencies or deadly systems of destruction [MIRV, ICBM] seem folksy, cute, and accessible" (par. 23). Any reader of Lasch's Vietnam-era essays will recognize the tone here. The range of illustrative allusions, from George Orwell to Walter Lippmann, from Abraham Lincoln to Henry James, from David Hume to T. H. Green, is also somehow his own, and helps give this opening chapter on punctuation its distinctive past-mindedness.

More distinctive still, however, is the chapter that follows, "Characteristics of Bad Writing." The opening epigraph from

Mather Byles had, after all, promised "an Ornament of a contrary Nature," namely, *The Art of Writing Incorrectly,* and it is here, as always, in telling us what has gone wrong, that Lasch's critical capacities come into their own. The chapter is, for starters, damn funny, as when Lasch, in admitting an important exception to the general rule of avoiding all forms of *to be*, imagines Hamlet asking himself "should I go on living or do away with myself" (par. 33), or when he rewrites the famous second paragraph of *The Education of Henry Adams*—"Had he been born in Jerusalem under the shadow of the Temple and circumcised in the Synagogues by his uncle the high priest . . ."—in the politically approved third person feminine (par. 42). The dangling modifier he found in Ernest Poole's novel *The Harbor*—"An enormous woman with heavy eyes, I was in awe of her from the first"—is priceless (par. 47), as is Woody Allen's satire on what Lasch calls the Hollywood but I would call the PBS/Ken Burns style of historical narration:

> 1738: Disowned, [the Earl of Sandwich] sets out for the Scandinavian countries, where he spends three years in intensive research on cheese. . . . Upon his return to England, he meets Nell Smallbore, a greengrocer's daughter, and they marry. She is to teach him all he will ever know about lettuce. (par. 46)

Those who knew Christopher Lasch only through his books, or who too readily accepted the received image of him as a dour, glowering Jeremiah, will perhaps be surprised to discover in these pages a different persona. Among family and friends, Lasch was a wry, playful, and whimsical man with a keen sense of fun. An imperfect Puritan, he loved cards, music, board games, charades, cocktails, and conversation, and at a time when he was intellectually at loose ends, unsure of where his serious work was going, *Plain Style* emerged out of this playful side of his nature. For all its ultimate seriousness of purpose, it was meant to be a lark.

Thus the almost fiendish delight Lasch takes in exposing the "dull, noun-heavy, Germanic prose churned out in such abundance by the academy." In most cases, he argues, the root of the trouble lies in the poverty of verbs, in the bad writer's almost exclusive reliance on (usually) abstract nouns and some form of the weak verb *to be*. Characterless and inactive, the verb *to be* in any of its forms — is, was, were, has been — takes all the life and spirit out of a sentence and leaves the reader gasping for direction (par. 33). Similarly inert and lifeless, the passive voice, for Lasch at least, also suggests a kind of moral cowardice insofar as it "disguises the subject and makes it hard to assign responsibility for an action." Thus its appeal to bureaucrats, "who wish to avoid responsibility for their decisions," and timid academics, who, unwilling to risk a straightforward judgment, unable, in fact, even to distinguish between judgment and prejudice, aspire above all else to "an appearance of detachment and objectivity" (par. 34). Note again the essentially democratic logic of these strictures. Lasch reviles such abstractions as *phenomena*, *socialization*, and *orientation* for their arrogant suggestion of "Olympian detachment from the commonplace facts of everyday life." Jargon he hates for its tendency to kill a general conversation. The whole unforgivable point of jargon, whether sociological, psychoanalytic, Marxist, structuralist, or poststructuralist, is, as he sees it, "to impress others with a display of special learning," "to identify the speaker as the possessor of secrets inaccessible to the multitude." Even mixed and hidden metaphors, which to most of us betray merely a moment's inattentiveness, suggest to Lasch something more disturbing: the severance of language from its roots in everyday experience. For him, the point of confining a word like *depend* as far as possible to its literal meaning (to hang from or hang down) was not to preserve the language in some sort of imagined original state, but rather to keep it in close relation to ordinary life.

In fact Lasch had no particular quarrel with the colloquial evolution of words. For him as for Orwell, the danger lay in the bureaucratization of language, not in its popularization. He ranged

astonishingly widely in finding his samples of bad writing, all the way from *TV Guide* to Thorstein Veblen and Herbert Croly. (Lasch was nothing if not fearless in taking on the great and the good — another populist impulse, and one surely meant to reassure students that even big shots could be bad writers.) On balance, though, it is fair to say that he scrutinized his corporate samples especially closely. In quoting the Miller Brewing Company's familiar advertising slogan for Lite Beer — "a third less calories than their regular beer" — he lets the colloquial substitution of *less* for *fewer* pass unnoticed for now, but condemns the plural pronoun *their* for its covert effort to make the company appear "just plain folks." Similarly, in the famous case of "Winston tastes good like a cigarette should," he rather imaginatively objects not just to the use of *like* as a conjunction but to the whole corporate ploy "to establish smoking as a kind of honorable American folkway." Those inclined to regard Lasch as a political apostate who threw over his Marxism in favor of conventional conservatism would do well to note these and other such passages. The Marxist idiom may be gone, replaced by a folk one, but the hostility to corporate capitalism abides as strong as ever before. A conservative Lasch may have become in the true, literal sense of the word, but a neoconservative never, as *Plain Style* helps make clear.

   In turning to "Words Often Misused" in Part IV, Lasch at once refers the reader to similar but more extensive lists in Strunk and White and Sheridan Baker. These were clearly his models and he saw no need to duplicate them. He did occasionally borrow from them, as when he quotes Strunk and White's useful illustration of the correct use of the word *comprise*, for instance (p. 96). But for the most part the list is his own, reflecting either new forms of misusage since their day (*access, impact, interface, point in time*) or Lasch's own abiding concerns as a thinker and historian (*competence, dependence, nostalgia, tradition*). The entries are usually short, pungent, and opinionated. Lasch hates the pretentious (*albeit*), the clinical (*behavior*), the trite (*bewildering variety*), the fancy (*com-*

prise), the literary (*dearth*), the cute (*enthuse*), the vague (*factor*), the lazy (*finalize*), the meaningless (*meaningful*), the highfalutin (*plethora*), the euphemistic (*problem*), the grotesque (*thusly*), and the gratuitous (*very*). He likes the humble (*although*), the domestic (*conduct*), the plain (*embrace*), the vernacular (*scarcity*), the homely (*carry on*), the direct (*part*), the vigorous (*end*), the ordinary (*excess*), the honest (*difficulty*), the simple (*so*), and the sparing. Some of his crotchets will strike readers as unreasonably censorious (*prior to*; *exploitative*). Certainly many of them are lost causes (*prestigious*). But we can only be grateful for the hopeful energy with which he attacks the constant misuse of, say, *disinterested*. Where Strunk and White are content wearily to point out that the word means "impartial," not "indifferent," Lasch delivers himself of a wry critical aside:

> Why does *disinterested* almost invariably show up, these days, when the speaker means *uninterested*? Probably because it sounds a little more imposing. Since most writers no longer know what *disinterested* means, they prefer it for that very reason, as a high-sounding substitute for the commonplace word designating boredom. Remember that disinterested inquiry — the ideal of scholarship — refers not to investigations conducted in a state of apathy or indifference but to a pursuit of truth so intense that it refuses to allow personal whim or inclination to interfere with the determination to follow an idea wherever it may lead. Disinterested inquiry signifies a refusal to indulge in wishful thinking. (p. 98)

Lasch's gloss on *problem* is probably his most characteristic: "Much overused, and misused as well, as a synonym for any kind of trouble, difficulty, mishap, obstacle, or misfortune — probably in conformity with the national belief that every untoward or unexpected turn of events has a simple solution" (p. 108). But for sheer

pith and brilliance nothing in *Plain Style* matches the priceless entry on *life style*:

> The appeal of this tired but now ubiquitous phrase probably lies in its suggestion that life is largely a matter of style. Find something else to say about life. (p. 104)

There you have, in the space of two sentences, both an astute diagnosis of the modern condition and a potent remedy for it — twenty-nine words that could change the world.

*   *   *

By late September 1985, having circulated a draft among his colleagues, accepted some suggestions for revision, and rejected others, Lasch had much more of a writing manual than he had originally planned: longer, more contentious, "but also more coherent and unified," he wrote, "in stressing certain central issues (such as the growing divorce between spoken and written speech), and (I hope) more sprightly and amusing." Hoping to avoid the expense of departmental publication, and thinking, moreover, "that the result of my labors may be of more general interest," he wrote to Edwin Barber at W. W. Norton on September 29 to broach the possibility of trade publication. The death of E. B. White two days later at age eighty-six must have struck him as poignantly coincident: he carefully preserved obituaries of White among his *Plain Style* papers. But Barber had no interest in anointing White's successor and declined *Plain Style* on the grounds that the market for such books was glutted.[47] A month later, Steven Fraser at Basic Books also declined, though he liked the book and offered to "sound things out" at Harper and Row (publishers of Baker's *Practical Stylist*) or the

---

47. Lasch to Edwin Barber (copy), 29 September 1985 (Lasch papers); Barber to Lasch, 15 October 1985 (Lasch papers).

University of Chicago Press (publishers of the *Chicago Manual of Style*) if Lasch wanted him to.[48] But by then not only was Lasch deep into his administrative responsibilities, he was also beginning to see his way clear toward a book on progress and its critics and ready to put *Plain Style* behind him. When I made my first visit to Rochester as a faculty candidate in November 1985, *Plain Style* was hot off the photocopier and had taken its assigned place atop the file cabinets in the history department office.

Lasch moved on. But as I noted at the outset, he never stopped tinkering with *Plain Style* in idle moments; it remained for a few more years at least a work in fitful progress. And he continued to brood on two developments in particular that boded further ill for the people's English.

The first of these was the computer. Lasch completed *Plain Style* just before the personal computer became the universal tool of composition. At the suggestion of colleagues more alert than he to the impending threat, he did include a late prohibition on *access* as a verb and on *interface* as anything at all. But the more baleful literary effects of the computer revolution still lay in the future when *Plain Style* went to press, as it were, in 1985. Lasch himself remained unacquainted with the computer until 1989, when at the request of his publisher he tried to shift the enormous, 250,000-word manuscript of *The True and Only Heaven* onto disks. Big mistake. Far from making things easier for him, the computer inevitably introduced new errors into what had been, he said, "a perfectly accurate text."[49] Lasch was no teary-eyed sentimentalist of pencil and paper, mind. Away from his desk he wrote on 8½-by-11-inch lined yellow legal pads in black, roller-ball ink. At his desk, he wrote directly on an IBM Selectric typewriter. In either case, however, he was *writing* and not, as the odious phrase has it, *word processing*. The trouble with the computer, as he came to see it, was not only that it intro-

48. Steven Fraser to Lasch, 19 November 1985 (Lasch papers).
49. Lasch to Jeannette Hopkins, 19 August 1989 (Hopkins papers).

duced a whole new field of compositional error—as when students persistently neglect to include page numbers on their papers, for instance, or when Microsoft Word obstinately refuses to place footnotes on the appropriate page—but that it seduced writers into a thoughtless and careless state of mind in which the machine is presumed to do all the work. At the end of his life, as he worked against time on the manuscript of *The Revolt of the Elites*, Lasch had reason to be grateful for the portable capacity of the laptop computer. But he remained wary of its corrupting influence on student writing especially. The very ease of production and revision that the computer allowed had, he knew, led students to think less about what they were doing and, consequently, write worse.

Mercifully, Lasch did not live to see the internet or the full digital revolution that the personal computer spawned. To watch a whole generation of supposed humanists trade in their wisdom and hard-earned knowledge for ready access to information would surely have sickened him.[50] But, sadly, he did live to see the same generation—or a sizable proportion of it—abandon the ideals of

50. "Unless information is generated by sustained public debate, most of it will be irrelevant at best, misleading and manipulative at worst," Lasch wrote in *The Revolt of the Elites*. He was thinking here of the useless, indigestible stuff churned out by press agencies and public relations bureaus and then regurgitated intact as "news" by such organs as *USA Today*. How much more useless and indigestible, though, is the unfiltered clutter generated by the internet, and how much more threatening to a culture of the word. "The most important effect of this obsession with information," Lasch wrote, in terms that recall the defining theme of *Plain Style*, "is to undermine the authority of the word. When words are used merely as instruments of publicity or propaganda, they lose their power to persuade. Soon they cease to mean anything at all. People lose the capacity to use language precisely and expressively or even to distinguish one word from another. The spoken word models itself on the written word instead of the other way around, and ordinary speech begins to sound like the clotted jargon we see in print. Ordinary speech begins to sound like 'information'—a disaster from which the English language may never recover" (Lasch, *The Revolt of the Elites and the Betrayal of American Democracy* [New York, 1995], 174–75).

disinterested scholarship and rational argument in favor of deliberately obscure and pointlessly political posturing. Again, let me make some important distinctions: Lasch was not a cultural reactionary driven to quivering, impotent rage by the assault of barbarian hordes on the western canon. (He admired the western canon, as it happens; he even thought it had something to offer men and women everywhere. But he knew that the canon wars that so convulsed a handful of campuses in the 1980s were "completely irrelevant to the plight of higher education as a whole."[51]) Nor was Lasch averse to theory in any stupidly predictable way. On the contrary, he had been among those calling for a more theoretically sophisticated approach to the writing of history since the late 1960s, and to the end he believed that historians should be fully conscious of their underlying assumptions about society and culture, less wholeheartedly empirical than they were often inclined to be, and more speculative, more willing to venture broad interpretive generalizations. What he saw too often by the 1980s, however, was theory standing in mindlessly for all the work of explanation, interpretation, and description. Postmodern theory of whatever variant had become, he thought, "the latest panacea, the latest source of ready-made answers, the latest substitute for thought."[52] It had also become the latest source of detestably bad writing. Theorists themselves, of course, and their slavish academic followers make this a political point of pride. Plain speech, in their view, is racist and phallocentric, an instrument of western or bourgeois oppression. Incomprehensible jargon, on the other hand, is the language of subversion and liberation. Needless to say, Lasch saw this for the career-driven, fashion-mongering pseudo-radicalism that it is, and at the end of his life, without ever succumbing to the embittered high-cultural conservatism of an Allan Bloom or Roger Kimball, he tried to recall historians to "the lost art of argument." For rea-

51. Lasch, *The Revolt of the Elites*, 171.
52. Blake and Phelps, "Conversations," 1324.

soned argument, argument understood not as "a clash of rival dogmas" or "a shouting match in which neither side gives any ground," but rather as "the attempt to bring others around to our own point of view," was, he felt, the essence of education and the surest sinew of American democracy.[53]

By the time his illness forced Lasch to give up the chairmanship of the history department at Rochester in the spring of 1993, he had more or less despaired of what passed for higher learning in the United States. The latest turgid monograph on the latest minute subject held not even passing interest for him. But he had enough faith in the common reader to push on, even beyond the eleventh hour, with *The Revolt of the Elites*, his final challenge to the smug complacencies of American privilege. And he retained a most unconventional respect and regard for his students, especially his undergraduate students, whose widely alleged apathy and political indifference struck him rather as a healthy radical skepticism. "I find this skepticism more attractive than not," Lasch said in his last departmental commencement address, "especially when contrasted to the ideological politics that have played such a prominent part in American life since the 1960s and are still pathetically playing themselves out, the second time as farce (as usual) in university departments of literary and cultural studies and other centers of the most self-consciously advanced academic thought." To be sure, radical skepticism sometimes ran the risk of cynicism. But what he sensed in his best students, Lasch said, was not cynicism but a "cold-eyed realism" by no means incompatible with warm and winning hearts. Teaching could be "a fairly discouraging business at times," he allowed,

> but just when you decide that it's all over with the life of
> the mind, that television has created a condition of terminal
> illiteracy, you find students (or rather they find you in some

53. Lasch, *The Revolt of the Elites*, 176.

miraculous way) who can read closely and carefully and write with enviable clarity and grace, sometimes in a voice that is already distinctively their own. And this voice can't possibly be described as the voice of cynicism and despair. . . . It's the voice of hope as distinguished from optimism. It's the voice, this new voice that I hear in the best of our students, of those who have a much better grasp than many of their so-called role models of the things that really matter in life — love, useful work, self-respect, honor, and integrity.[54]

Honor and integrity, clarity and grace: for thirty-five years, these were the plain, reciprocal qualities that Christopher Lasch brought to bear on his own useful work, and now, nearly a decade from his death, we stand in greater need of them than ever.

54. Lasch, "The Baby Boomers: Here Today, Gone Tomorrow: Commencement Address to the Department of History at the University of Rochester, Spring 1993," *New Oxford Review* (September 1993): 7–8, 10.

A Note on the Text

This first published edition of *Plain Style* is based on a revised typescript found among the Christopher Lasch papers at the University of Rochester. Approximately 10 percent longer than the original typescript that Lasch reproduced for use in the history department in 1985, it dates, I believe, to 1986 or 1987. After that time, Lasch continued to make fragmentary handwritten revisions to what was clearly a working typescript, and these I have completed and included here whenever I could unmistakably discern his intention. Throughout the text, I have corrected typographical errors and misquotations and updated references to current editions of Strunk and White and the *Chicago Manual of Style*. Occasionally I have altered Lasch's placement of material in the interests of clarity and utility. But I have resisted the temptation to bring *Plain Style* up to date either by adding new entries addressed to new forms of misusage or by excising those few technical, editorial entries (on word division at the end of the line, for instance) that in the age of the personal computer may strike some readers as obsolete. In time, one may well want to do this so that *Plain Style* will remain the immediately serviceable book that Lasch meant it to be. But for now, let it appear as he left it in deference to his efforts of not so very long ago.

I

Elementary Principles of
Literary Construction

Since the sentence is the basic unit of literary composition, an introduction to style will have to give most of its attention to the misunderstandings, sloppy habits, and misplaced eloquence that lead to ill-formed, tone-deaf, ambiguous, or downright unreadable sentences. Even those who can write a passable sentence, however, often find it beyond their power to arrange sentences so that one follows another in a logical order. To construct a coherent paragraph, let alone a coherent essay, dissertation, or monograph, exceeds their command of language. It seems essential, therefore, to begin this manual with a few observations about the elements of composition.

These elements cannot be reduced to a recipe. It is nevertheless helpful to bear in mind that every composition, whatever its length, ought to have a beginning, a middle, and an end. This deceptively simple observation will yield some insight into the art of composition if we consider some of its implications.

A beginning does not consist of an announcement of the author's intentions, a preview of coming attractions. Here is an example of how not to begin:

> In this paper, I will examine some of the characteristics of the undergraduate mind. Teachers often complain that undergraduates have no interest in ideas and that their minds are completely unformed. I will try to show that undergraduates come to college, on the contrary, with very definite though largely unconscious ideas about life. This unconscious philosophy, I will argue, is completely at odds with the critical and scientific culture of the college itself. I will conclude by arguing that instead of recognizing the disparity between the sporting culture of undergraduates and the scientific ideals that govern higher learning, the college makes so many concessions to the sporting ideal that it never challenges the students intellectually or forces them to grow up.

This lacks for nothing in clarity; yet it does not provide a forceful beginning (see par. 38, *Unnecessary Preliminaries*). What the reader wants to know is not what you plan to say but where you stand. He needs some assurance that your point of view promises fresh illumination. He listens to your tone of voice, which conveys your intentions more quickly and clearly than a summary outline of the forthcoming composition. A vigorous introduction, therefore, will seek to establish not so much the subject matter to be addressed as the author's way of addressing it. It will announce or at least prefigure the argument the author plans to pursue.

In order to illustrate these points, to show how the beginning of a composition leads to a middle and thence to an appropriate ending, and to show, moreover, that these principles ought to govern even a very short composition, we have reproduced here a 1,500-word essay by Randolph Bourne, a master of the short essay. "The Undergraduate," originally published in the *New Republic* for 25 September 1915, is by no means a dazzling piece of work, but it is eminently competent and self-assured, and it makes its modest point with a good deal of authority. Let us see how Bourne proceeds.

The Undergraduate

RANDOLPH BOURNE

[1] In these days of academic self-analysis, the intellectual caliber of the American undergraduate finds few admirers or defenders. Professors speak resignedly of the poverty of his background and imagination. Even the undergraduate himself in college editorials confesses that the student soul vibrates reluctantly to the larger intellectual and social issues of the day. The absorption in petty gossip, sports, class politics, fraternity life, suggests that too many undergraduates regard their college in light of a glorified preparatory school where the activities of their boyhood may be worked out on a grandiose scale. They do not act as if they thought of the college as a new intellectual society in which one acquired certain rather definite scientific and professional attitudes, and learned new interpretations which threw experience and information into new terms and new lights. The average undergraduate tends to meet studies like philosophy, psychology, economics, general history, with a frankly puzzled wonder. A whole new world seems to dawn on him, in its setting and vocabulary alien to anything in his previous life. Every teacher knows this baffling resistance of the undergraduate mind.

[2] It is not so much that the student resists facts and details. He will absorb trusts and labor unions, municipal government and direct primaries, the poems of Matthew Arnold, and James's theory of the emotions. There is no unkindliness of his mind towards fairly concrete material. What he is more or less impervious to is points-of-view, interpretations. He seems to lack philosophy. The college has to let too many undergraduates pass out into professional and business life, not only without the germ of a philosophy, but without any desire for an interpretative clue through the

maze. In this respect the American undergraduate presents a distinct contrast to the European. For the latter does seem to get a certain intellectual setting for his ideas which makes him intelligible, and gives journalism and the ordinary expression of life a certain tang which we lack here. Few of our undergraduates get from the college any such intellectual impress.

[3] The explanation is probably not that the student has no philosophy, but that he comes to college with an unconscious philosophy so tenacious that the four years of the college in its present technique can do little to disintegrate it. The cultural background of the well-to-do American home with its "nice" people, its sentimental fiction and popular music, its amiable religiosity and vague moral optimism, is far more alien to the stern secular realism of modern university teaching than most people are willing to admit. The college world would find itself less frustrated by the undergraduate's secret hostility if it would more frankly recognize what a challenge its own attitudes are to our homely American ways of thinking and feeling. Since the college has not felt this dramatic contrast, or at least has not felt a holy mission to assail our American mushiness of thought through the undergraduate, it has rather let the latter run away with the college.

[4] It is a trite complaint that the undergraduate takes his extracurricular activities more seriously than his studies. But he does this because his homely latent philosophy is essentially a sporting philosophy, the good old Anglo-Saxon conviction that life is essentially a game whose significance lies in terms of winning or losing. The passion of the American undergraduate for intercollegiate athletics is merely a symbol of a general interpretation for all the activities that

come to his attention. If he is interested in politics, it is in election campaigns, in the contests of parties and personalities. His parades and cheerings are the encouragement of a racer for the goal. After election, his enthusiasm collapses. His spiritual energy goes into class politics, fraternity and club emulation, athletics, every activity which is translatable into terms of winning and losing. In Continental universities this energy would go rather into a turbulence for causes and ideas, a militant radicalism or even a more militant conservatism that would send Paris students out into the streets with a "Caillaux assassin!" or tie up an Italian town for the sake of *Italia irredenta*. Even the war, though it has called out a fund of anti-militarist sentiment in the American colleges, still tends to be spoken of in terms of an international sporting event. "Who will win?" is the question here.

[5] Now this sporting philosophy by which the American undergraduate lives, and which he seems to bring with him from his home, may be a very good philosophy for an American. It is of the same stuff with our good-humored contempt for introspection, our dread of the "morbid," our dislike of conflicting issues and insoluble problems. The sporting attitude is a grateful and easy one. Issues are decided cleanly. No irritating fringes are left over. The game is won or lost. Analysis and speculation seem superfluous. The point is that such a philosophy is as different as possible from that which motivates the intellectual world of the modern college, with its searchings, its hypotheses and interpretations and revisions, its flexibility and openness of mind. In the scientific world of the instructor, things are not won or lost. His attitude is not a sporting one.

[6] Yet the college has allowed some of these sporting attitudes to be imposed upon it. The undergraduates' gladia-

torial contests proceed under faculty supervision and patronage. Alumni contribute their support to screwing up
athletic competition to the highest semi-professional pitch.
They lend their hallowing patronage to fraternity life and
other college institutions which tend to emphasize social
distinction. And the college administration, in contrast to
the European scheme, has turned the college course into a
sort of race with a prize at the goal. The degree has become
a sort of honorific badge for all classes of society, and the
colleges have been forced to give it this quasi-athletic setting and fix the elaborate rules of the game by which it may
be won—rules which shall be easy enough to get all classes
competing for it, and hard enough to make it a sufficient
prize to keep them all in the race. An intricate system of
points and courses and examinations sets the student working for marks and the completion of schedules rather than
for a new orientation in important fields of human interest.

[7] The undergraduate can scarcely be blamed for respond-
ing to a system which so strongly resembles his sports, or for
bending his energies to playing the game right, rather than
assimilating the intellectual background of his teachers. So
strongly has this sporting technique been acquired by the
college that even when the undergraduate lacks the sporting
instinct and does become interested in ideas, he is apt to find
that he has only drawn attention to his own precocity and
won amused notice rather than respect. In spite of the desire
of instructors to get themselves over to their students, in
spite of a real effort to break down the "class-consciousness"
of teacher and student, the gulf between their attitudes is
too fundamental to be easily bridged. Unless it is bridged,
however, the undergraduate is left in a sort of Peter Pan
condition, looking back to his schoolboy life and carrying
along his schoolboy interests with him, instead of anticipat-

ing his graduate or professional study or his active life. What should be an introduction to professional or business life in a world of urgent political and social issues, and the acquiring of intellectual tools with which to meet their demands, becomes a sort of sequestered retreat out of which to jump from boyhood into a badly prepared middle age.

[8] The college will not really get the undergraduate until it becomes more conscious of the contrast of its own philosophy with his sporting philosophy, and tackles his boyish Americanisms less mercifully, or until it makes college life less like that of an undergraduate country club, and more of an intellectual workshop where men and women in the fire of their youth, with conflicts and idealism, questions and ambitions and desire for expression, come to serve an apprenticeship under the masters of the time.

Note that Bourne plunges right into his subject—the "intellectual caliber" of the American undergraduate—without preliminary explanations, fanfare, or apologies. The very first paragraph accomplishes several important things in a highly economical and unobtrusive fashion. By recalling a number of familiar, uncontroversial facts, acknowledged by students and professors alike, Bourne manages to draw readers into his argument by confronting them with a description of the world that is immediately recognizable. At the same time, he intimates that this description is incomplete, precisely because it is so familiar. Everyone knows that undergraduates resist education. The question is what underlies this resistance.

In the second paragraph, Bourne refines and complicates the description offered in the first paragraph. What students resist, he adds, is not "facts and details" but "interpretations." This new consideration prompts a provisional explanation of the impasse in the classroom, or at least a more precise characterization of the "undergraduate mind." The undergraduate, Bourne proposes, "seems to lack philosophy."

The third paragraph, which still belongs to the beginning of the essay but provides a bridge to the middle section, proceeds immediately to a further qualification, which amounts to a correction of the superficial generalization that undergraduates have no philosophy. What they have, it now appears, is an unconscious philosophy, one derived from the "cultural background of the well-to-do American home"; and the most important point about this sentimental, undemanding view of life, as Bourne sees it (the most important point, anyway, for the purposes of the present essay), is that it finds itself completely at odds with the "stern secular realism of modern university teaching." Here Bourne announces his central theme: the contrast between the "vague moral optimism" of middle America (as it would be called today) and the critical spirit that informs modern scientific, philosophical, and literary speculation.

In the next two paragraphs, the heart of the essay, Bourne offers a fuller account of the undergraduate's "homely latent philosophy." This philosophy rests on a sporting view of life, the implications of which Bourne proceeds to make explicit—among them, and most important, the assumption that all "issues are decided cleanly." Once the matter is stated in this way, we see more clearly why the sporting culture conflicts with the "scientific world of the instructor," in which nothing is ever decided cleanly and every conclusion is provisional and subject to revision.

The last three paragraphs, which constitute a concluding section, grow out of the further twist in the argument accomplished by the sixth paragraph, which shifts the reader's attention from the "undergraduate mind" to the college itself and blames the college, not the undergraduate, for the sorry state of higher education. Instead of resisting the sporting view of life, according to Bourne, the college institutionalizes it in the form of grades, schedules, and other "quasi-athletic" academic rituals. This contention can be regarded as Bourne's major conclusion. In other words, it represents the climax of his argument; and this is what is meant by a conclusion, not a summary in which the writer tries to round things off by repeating the same uninformative outline with which he began.

The difference between a conclusion and a summary is further illustrated by the last paragraph of Bourne's essay, in which the conclusion itself undergoes modification. Not only does the college reinforce the sporting view of experience, according to Bourne, but it does not even recognize the "contrast of its own philosophy with the undergraduate's sporting philosophy." This final consideration firmly but inconspicuously caps and justifies everything that has led up to it. The purpose of the essay lies in the exposure of what was hitherto concealed, namely the "philosophical" or ideological basis of the tension between university undergraduates and their teachers. It is the unacknowledged opposition between two different ways of thinking about the world, according to Bourne, that explains "this baffling resistance of the undergraduate mind."

This artful little essay shows how a great deal of fairly complex argumentation can be contained in a small compass, without any ostentatious display of erudition, without the usual spiteful attacks on the work of other authorities in the field, without elaborate preliminaries or tedious summations, and without the crablike sideways motion and backtracking that so often characterize the work of inexperienced writers. Every point leads logically to the next, and every paragraph, every sentence even, adds something to the last, carrying the argument firmly forward to a conclusion that seems both effortless and irresistible because it has been so carefully prepared.

II

Conventions Governing Punctuation, Capitalization, Typography, and Footnotes

1. **Serial Commas**   Use a comma before the last item in a series. This practice is now almost universally preferred, at least in the United States, to the older practice, which omits the comma when the last two items in a series are joined by a conjunction.

> Instead of speaking abstractly of the need for sacrifice, Winston Churchill used more concrete and therefore more vivid and memorable language: blood, toil, tears, and sweat.

2. **Breathing Spaces**   A comma, it should be remembered, indicates a short pause or breathing space. As writing becomes more and more remote from spoken language, it takes an effort to recall such elementary uses of punctuation, which also govern the use of semicolons, parentheses, and dashes. These marks indicate progressively more radical interruptions in the flow of thought. Precisely because all these punctuation marks do interrupt the flow of thought, it is tempting to state it as a general principle that they should be used as sparingly as possible. Some such unstated

principle, in fact, seems to underlie modern typographical practice, which has moved steadily away from the ornate punctuation, the prolific use of commas, the ever-ready resort to the dash, and the superabundance of typographical symbols of all sorts that characterized written English in the eighteenth and early nineteenth centuries. This simplification is not an unambiguously desirable development. It has encouraged, among other things, a serious underuse of the comma, a useful symbol the existence of which many novices, and many professional writers as well, particularly journalists, seem to have irretrievably forgotten.

Recent typographical practice betrays its indifference to the requirements of spoken English in its inconsistency. The same journalists, ad writers, copy editors, and composition instructors who demand the elimination of "unnecessary" commas, even in sentences where they serve a useful purpose, pedantically insist on a comma after an introductory *but*, *yet*, or *thus*:

> Yet, the most carefully laid plans go awry. (*Wrong-headed and tone-deaf*)

The comma serves no purpose in such constructions except to call attention to itself, as if to compensate for its elimination in cases where it is really needed.

3. Compound Sentences and Compound Predicates The clauses of a compound sentence (which consists of two or more independent clauses each with its own subject and verb) should be separated by a comma. A compound predicate (two or more verbs) having the same subject does not require a comma.

> George Orwell still considered himself a socialist when he wrote *1984*, but *Life* and *Time* hailed the novel as a condemnation of socialism.

> Only a few years before, *Life* had extolled the Russians as "one hell of a people" and refused to serialize Walter

Lippmann's *U.S. War Aims* on the grounds that it was "too anti-Russian."

4. Commas in Relative Clauses   Note the punctuation of these sentences:

The blizzard of 1967, which lasted for three days and left more than three feet of snow on the ground, surpassed any other storm in recent years.

The hand that rocks the cradle rules the world.

In the first sentence, the (nonrestrictive) clause introduced by *which* adds something to the blizzard but does not restrict or qualify its meaning. It is a parenthetical expression, in effect; as such, it is set off by commas. In the second sentence, the clause introduced by *that* is restrictive; it distinguishes *the hand* from some other hand. Because it is an integral part of the sentence, not merely an addition or afterthought, it is not set off by commas. For further discussion of this point, see *that, which* (pp. 109–10, below).

5. Semicolons in Compound Sentences   Use a semicolon to separate the clauses of a compound sentence when they are not connected by a conjunction or when they are connected by an adverb like *thus*.

George Orwell considered himself a socialist; the American press made him a hero of the free world in its struggle against socialism.

In the sixties, the public schools began to emphasize "concepts" and "problems" in the teaching of history; thus many students now graduate from high school with only a tenuous grasp of historical facts.

6. Commas and Semicolons with Quotation Marks Commas should be placed inside quotation marks, semicolons outside:

Although Dr. Pangloss insists that we live in the "best of all possible worlds," Candide's experience leads him to a very different conclusion.

Pangloss thinks he lives in the "best of all possible worlds"; Candide, learning better, decides to cultivate his own garden.

7. Plurals   English plurals are formed by adding *s* or *es*, and this rule applies to proper nouns as well as to common nouns.

If an apple a day keeps the doctor away, how many doctors will a dozen apples keep away?

Keeping up with the Joneses is hard work.

Quentin could live with one Snopes at a time but found a whole clan of Snopeses unbearable.

One Garvey is an all-star first baseman; two Garveys make a model couple.

8. Possessives as Distinguished from Plurals   Enormous confusion, in this age of semi-literacy, surrounds the use of the apostrophe. The basic rule is simple. The apostrophe designates a possessive, not a plural. English plurals, as noted, are formed by adding an *s*, not by adding an *s* together with a superfluous apostrophe. Thus the plural form of *animal* is *animals*, not *animals'*, and the plural form of *Garvey* is *Garveys*, not *Garveys'*.

Confusion arises because the letter *s* designates both the plural form of most nouns and (with an apostrophe) the possessive form of singular nouns. Because the letter *s* often appears in conjunction with an apostrophe (in possessives, that is, like *Paul's case* or *the rabbit's revenge*), those who do not grasp the grammatical principle at stake jump to the conclusion that it must never appear without this absurd little escort. As a result, such monstrosities as these leer at us around every corner:

The two wayward rabbits' decided to get even with
Mr. McGregor by invading his garden. (*Incorrect*)

The Garveys' decided to get a divorce and thereby dismayed
many of their fans. (*Incorrect*)

The first thing to remember, then, is that the apostrophe designates
the possessive form, never the plural form of a noun.

The animals decided to take over the farm. (*Plural*)

The animals' revolt ended in the reestablishment of autoc-
racy under the guise of egalitarianism. (*Possessive*)

Sportswriters and gossip columnists portrayed the Garveys
as a model couple, an inspiration to clean-living Americans
everywhere. (*Plural*)

The Garveys' divorce put an end to all that. (*Possessive*)

9. Possessives of Singular Nouns Ending in *s* Further confusion about the use of apostrophes, not unrelated to the confusion
about plural nouns, arises out of singular nouns ending in *s*, often
mistakenly treated as if they were plurals:

Lois' big mistake (write: *Lois's* big mistake)

the darkness' mystery (write: the *darkness's* mystery)

Confusion can be avoided only by mastering the basic rule, which
is clear and simple. The possessive form of singular nouns is formed
by adding an apostrophe, followed by an *s* (blindman's buff; the
plaintiff's argument; Bonnie's unfailing good humor). When a singular noun ends in *s*, the possessive is still formed in exactly the
same way.

Henry James's convoluted later style

Silas's rise and fall

In spite of the simplicity of the underlying rules governing plurals and possessives, things have now reached the point where many people, hopelessly confused about the use of the apostrophe, omit it altogether, just as they have gradually divested their writing of commas.

> The darkness mystery has always appealed to poets. (*Incorrect*)

> The Garveys divorce put an end to all that. (*Incorrect*)

> The animals revolt ended badly. (*Incorrect*)

This will not do at all.

10. Apostrophes in Contractions   The apostrophe (one use of which is described in pars. 8 and 9) has a second use. Besides designating possessives, it also designates a missing letter in contractions, and the misuse of the apostrophe in plurals may derive, in part, from a tendency to confuse these two parts of speech.

> Steve Garvey's a mighty fine first baseman. (*Contraction*)

> Garvey's life-time batting average is nothing to sneer at. (*Singular possessive*)

> As a model couple, the Garveys did not escape the sneers of sophisticated cynics. (*Plural*)

> The Garveys' finest moment as a couple, according to scoffers, was their uncoupling. (*Plural possessive*)

In the first of these four sentences, the proper noun appears as a contraction, with the apostrophe substituting for the missing letter in the verb *is*. In the second sentence, the proper noun appears in the singular possessive form. In the third sentence, it has become a plural, while in the fourth, the addition of a final apostrophe transforms the plural into a possessive.

In general, contractions should not appear at all in formal writing, even in formal writing that seeks to remain as colloquial and plain as possible. A breezy style full of contractions is by no means the same thing as a plain style, as can be seen in this excerpt from one of Pauline Kael's movie reviews in the *New Yorker*, where contractions mingle with the aesthetic, therapeutic idiom of jaded urban sophistication ("reemphasizes the irony," "vocally bland," "totally lacking," "neurotic strength," "semblance of believability"):

> In the last scene, . . . she's fake naïve, and the material defeats her: it reemphasizes the irony of Susan's blasted hopes which we've already gnawed on for two hours. For the rest, she's proficient, yet vocally bland and totally lacking in the neurotic strength that might lend the role a semblance of believability.

11. Compound Words   According to the editors of the *Chicago Manual of Style*, the use of a hyphen in compound words generates more uncertainty than any other question of punctuation or typography. In general, the trend is away from the hyphen—probably not an entirely desirable trend, since it encourages a Germanic piling up of nouns on nouns and perhaps also, more obscurely, a style of writing that accentuates nouns instead of verbs. In the best English writing, on the other hand, verbs, not nouns, tend to occupy the central position in the structure of sentences (see par. 32, *Nouns and Verbs*). On compound words, see the *Chicago Manual of Style*, 14th edition (1993), pars. 6.32–6.42.

Compound words often appear as adjectives, in which case they should almost always be hyphenated. *Middle class*, for example, should be written without a hyphen when it appears as a noun, but it should be hyphenated when it appears as an adjective.

> The rise of the middle class can explain almost any historical event.

> Historians have argued endlessly about the middle-class origins of the English revolution.

Proper nouns, however, are not hyphenated when used as adjectives. Write "the Home Rule Bill, not "the Home-Rule Bill"; "the *New York Times*," not "the *New-York Times*."

In doubtful cases, readability and familiarity can resolve the question of whether to run two words together or to connect them with a hyphen. *Semicolon* is so easily recognizable that *semi-colon* seems pedantic; but *semi-literacy* is preferable to *semiliteracy* for the same reason that Dan Jenkins entitled his novel *Semi-Tough*, not *Semitough*—a compound hard to decipher at first glance.

H. W. Fowler's long entry (in his *Modern English Usage*) provides a useful guide to the finer points of hyphenation, though not always to current usage. Fowler still hyphenates many compound words now printed as one word: *blackbird*, *redcoat*. But he explains very clearly the instructive difference between a *black bird* and a *black-bird* (or *blackbird*) and between a *red coat* and a *redcoat*.

12. Double Quotation Marks   All quoted material, except for long indented quotations (see par. 14) and quotations within quotations (see par. 13), should be enclosed within *double* quotation marks. This rule applies to short phrases as well as to complete sentences. For some reason, many writers now labor under the misunderstanding that double quotation marks are to be used only for lengthy excerpts, while single words or short phrases are to be announced by single quotation marks. The only basis for this curious belief is the "convention in works of philosophy and theology," as the *Chicago Manual of Style* puts it, that "terms having special philosophical or theological meaning are often enclosed in single quotation marks." The same authority contends that "in linguistic and phonetic studies a word under discussion is often set in italics . . . and the definition enclosed in single quotation marks, with no intervening punctuation" (pars. 6.67, 6.74). The authors of the *Chicago Manual* do not confront the objection that double quotation marks would serve the purpose just as well, nor do they explain why single quotation marks should not *invariably* appear in these technical contexts. The qualification that they "often" appear indicates that this typographical practice remains discretionary. The reason it has not become universal, presumably, is that it makes so little sense. Not only does it involve writers and editors in endless niggling decisions about whether a word in any given passage carries some "special philosophical or theological meaning," it ignores the obvious fact that double quotation marks themselves indicate, among other things, that words are being used in some special sense. This fine distinction in the use of double and single quotation marks proves not only unworkable but unnecessary as well. The attempt to maintain it, moreover, encourages the nervous, self-conscious use of quotation marks that afflicts so much academic writing (see par. 16, *Excessive Use of Quotation Marks and Other Visual Aids*).

One other possible source of confusion should be mentioned. British typographical practice reverses American practice. It uses single quotation marks where American practice dictates double quotations marks, and vice versa.

> Alasdair MacIntyre has written, with reference to Hume, that 'as shared ideals and accepted functions drop away in the age of individualism, the injunctions (of morality, that is) have less and less backing. The end of this process is the appearance of a "you ought . . ." unbacked by reasons, announcing traditional moral rules in a vacuum . . .' (*British typographical practice*)

In this example, the double quotation marks designate a quotation within the larger quotation enclosed within single quotation marks (see par. 13, *Quotations Within Quotations*). The passage would be Americanized as follows:

> Alasdair MacIntyre has written, with reference to Hume, that "as shared ideals and accepted functions drop away in the age of individualism, the injunctions (of morality, that is) have less and less backing. The end of this process is the appearance of a 'you ought . . .' unbacked by reasons, announcing traditional moral rules in a vacuum . . ." (*American typographical practice*)

Another example will show how exposure to British practice may contribute to the prevailing confusion about single and double quotation marks.

> T. H. Green . . . asserted the mutual dependence of society and the 'individual', or 'persons'; while Hobhouse, similarly, asserted that 'freedom is only one side of social life', and that 'the theory of collective action' was 'no less fundamental than the theory of personal freedom'. (*British practice*)

A reader who encounters a string of words and short phrases enclosed in single quotation marks, in a British book, may jump to the conclusion that words and short phrases must always be punctuated in this way. In American practice, however, all the words and phrases in this passage would be enclosed in double quotation marks, whether or not some of them may be used in some "special philosophical or theological" sense.

13. Quotations Within Quotations   These should be enclosed within single quotation marks.

> In order to illustrate the bureaucratization of language, Orwell translated a verse from Ecclesiastes into "modern English of the worst sort." He could not make an exact translation, he explained, because concrete allusions to races, battles, and bread had to be dissolved "into the vague phrase 'success or failure in competitive activities'." "This had to be so, because . . . no one capable of using phrases like 'objec-

tive consideration of contemporary phenomena' would ever tabulate his thoughts" in the "precise and detailed" language of the King James Bible.

14. Indented Quotations   Quotations should be set off from the rest of the text (indented) only when they run to eight or ten typewritten lines. Do *not* use quotation marks to introduce indented quotations or block quotations, as printers call them. Indentation serves in lieu of quotation marks. If quotation marks appear within the quoted material, use double quotation marks, not single ones, as you would in quotations in the text (par. 13). If the indented quotation is run into the preceding sentence of the text, do not begin the quotation with a capital letter, even if the original was a complete sentence beginning with a capital.

> Lincoln's eloquence remains undimmed by the happy falsification of his prediction that
>> the world will little note, nor long remember what we say here. . . . It is . . . for us [he continued] to be here dedicated to the great task remaining before us [and to] resolve that these dead shall not have died in vain—that this nation, under God, shall have a new birth of freedom—and that government of the people, by the people, for the people, shall not perish from the earth.

It is a good idea to avoid long quotations, especially quotations long enough to require indentation. There are few such quotations in academic writing that could not better be paraphrased. Long quotations not only discourage the reader, they often serve as a substitute for thought on the part of the writer. Try to quote partial sentences and to work these into your own sentences. The *Chicago Manual* says wisely that the "skill with which fragmentary quotations are incorporated into a text" will reflect "an author's awareness of syntax, verb tenses, personal pronouns," and the grammatical structure both of his own writing and of the writing he quotes (par. 10.12).

15. Alterations in Quoted Material   Note the use of ellipses in the indented quotation in par. 14. Three dots indicate an omission within a sentence. Four dots—a period, followed by three spaced dotes—indicate the omission of the last part of the quoted sentence. Whenever four dots are used, the following sentence should begin with a capital, whether or not it is the beginning of a sentence in the quoted text. It is now considered pedantic to indicate such minor alterations in punctuation, introduced for the sake of readability, by putting the capital letters in brackets.

The addition of italics, however, must be scrupulously acknowledged, either in the body of the quotation (in brackets) or in a footnote, by the expression "italics mine" or "italics added." Sometimes it may also be necessary to indicate that the italics appear in the original. The expression *sic* (*thus* or *so*) may be used to indicate some misspelling or error in the original. Overuse of this device and of other typographical devices, however, is to be avoided.

16. Excessive Use of Quotation Marks and Other Visual Aids   Quotation marks, like italics and other typographical devices, should be used sparingly. Let the words themselves—the structure and rhythm of sentences, the arrangement of sentences in relation to each other, the organization of paragraphs—carry your meaning, without visual aids. Academic writers too easily become addicted to the use of quotation marks, whether to signify irony and sarcasm, to establish a certain lofty distance from the commonplace facts of everyday life, to imply that ordinary terms are being used in an unfamiliar and esoteric way, or perhaps also to confess the writer's inability to say anything in a straightforward way. Talcott Parsons—to cite only one among many offenders—was a master of pointless quotation marks.

The child, from the beginning, is to some degree an active agent who "tries" to do things and—increasingly with time—is rewarded or punished according to his "success" in doing them. The mother, on her side, actively manipulates the situation in which this learning takes place. . . . She determines the "picking up" and the "setting down" of the baby, . . . and so on.

The use of italics for emphasis can easily become addictive, as in J. D. Salinger's *Catcher in the Rye*:

I kept hoping it wasn't *my* door they were knocking on, but I knew damn well it was. I don't know *how* I knew, but I knew. I knew *who* it was, too. I'm psychic.

Salinger is attempting, of course, to convey his narrator's verbal mannerisms. Even so, it is debatable whether the italics add much to these sentences. If the reader can't be trusted to get the point without underlining it or putting it in quotation marks, the author probably needs to express it more clearly.

17. **Foreign Words**   Italicize foreign words and expressions when they are isolated in an English sentence. Do not italicize entire foreign sentences. In general, the use of foreign words should be kept to a minimum. Use them only when you can't find an exact English equivalent—not to give an air of learning and elegance.

18. **Italicized Titles.**   Italicize titles of books, newspapers, and periodicals. Titles of movies, paintings, and long poems should also be italicized. Titles of dissertations, theses, and unpublished scholarly papers should be set in roman type and enclosed in quotation marks. The same goes for articles, chapters in a book, and short poems.

19. Dashes   Like quotation marks and italics, dashes should be used sparingly. In typewritten manuscripts, the dash is indicated by a double hyphen. In printers' terminology, this symbol is known as a one-em dash (because it occupies the same amount of space as the letter m) and written ⫣, to distinguish it from a one-en dash, which is used principally with numbers (e.g., 1968–72). In typescripts, no distinction is made between a one-en dash and a hyphen.

20. Word Division   When dividing words at the end of a line, divide them between syllables according to pronunciation.

> democ-racy (*not* demo-cracy)

> knowl-edge (*not* know-ledge)

Divisions should be made after a vowel, in most cases.

> criti-cism (*not* crit-icism)

> physi-cal (*not* phys-ical)

Words ending in *ing* should be divided before the final *ing*, unless they contain a doubled consonant, in which case the added consonant is carried over to the next line.

> certify-ing   giv-ing   improvis-ing

> bid-ding   control-ling   trip-ping

21. Abbreviations   Except for such familiar expressions as A.D., B.C., A.M., and P.M., abbreviations should not be used in the body of the text. Even in footnotes, many publishers now prefer to write out the names of months, say, in dates and citations. Expressions like *e.g.* (*exempli gratia*, for example), *i.e.*, (*id est*, that is), *etc.* (*et cetera*, and so on), and *et al.* (*et alii*, and others), fall under the ban on the use of abbreviations in the running text. These and a number of other abbreviations, however, often appear in footnotes, notably *ca.* or *c.* (*circa*, about or approximately), *cf.* (*confer*, compare), *et seq.* (*et sequentes*, and the following), *ibid.* (*ibidem*, in the same place), *loc. cit.* (*loco citato*, in the place cited), N. B. (*nota bene*, note well), *op. cit.* (*opere citato*, in the work cited), *pass.* (*passim*, throughout), *q.v.* (*quod vide*, which see), *sup.* (*supra*, above), *v.* (*vide*, see), and *viz.* (*videlicet*, namely). There is much uncertainty as to whether such abbreviations of Latin words should be written in italics. Some publishers prefer roman type. The important thing is consistency.

For the use of *ibid.*, *loc. cit.*, and *op. cit.*, see also par. 30.

22. Postal Abbreviations   Do not use the new postal abbreviations either in the running text or in footnotes. The old abbreviations—Mass., Miss.—are sanctified by custom. The new ones—MA, MS—are bureaucratic innovations designed to surround the postal service with an illusory air of efficiency. Accordingly they fall under the general prohibition of bureaucratic speech and writing, the invariable purpose of which is evasion and obfuscation, even when it appears, as here, to signal the streamlined, computerized elimination of waste motion.

23. Initials of Organizations, Bureaucratic Agencies, and Weapons Systems.   In accordance with the principle that good writing must always oppose the bureaucratic debasement of language, it is a good idea, wherever possible, to refer to the names of governmental agencies, voluntary associations, and other organizations by their full name, not by their initials. The widespread use of initials tends either to lend suspect purposes a spurious air of importance and dignity or, as in the now almost mandatory resort to acronyms in naming organizations, agencies, and weapons systems (MIRV, SALT, PAWS [Phased Array Warning System], TACAMO [Take Charge and Move Out]), to make remote bureaucratic agencies or deadly systems of destruction seem folksy, cute, and accessible. Good writing should resist such designs, although there are obvious limits beyond which it is not possible to avoid initials. A historian of the New Deal, say, will find it impossible to refer again and again to the National Recovery Administration (NRA), the Tennessee Valley Authority (TVA), and the Temporary National Economic Committee (TNEC). In such cases, a good rule is to spell the whole thing out when it first appears, adding initials in parentheses, and then to use only the initials in subsequent references.

Russell Baker suggests "two possible explanations" for the "trend that is reducing English to an alphabetic breeze." One is that "expansive technology, science, and government have overloaded the language with so many big, hard-to-remember, hard-to-pronounce words that the substitution of a shorthand language is inevitable." The other is a "mischievous impulse" among "eggheads, who create most of this alphabet talk, to resist the calcification of the language by keeping it as breezy as a tabloid headline." Either way, he adds, "the old mother tongue is anything but A-O.K. and getting murkier every day."

24. Capitalization   Capitalize *Western Europe, Eastern Europe*, and similar expressions when they refer to political as opposed to merely geographical divisions. The general trend in current usage favors more and more sparing use of capitals. German nouns, however, should always be capitalized, including such supposedly naturalized ones as *Führer*.

> Know-Nothing party
> Republican party
> progressive movement (*but* Progressive party)
> eighteenth century
> the twenties
> *quattrocento*
> the North, the South (*but* southern United States)
> industrial revolution

French revolution
westward movement
Catholic church

25. Numbers   Numbers of less than one hundred should be spelled out; numbers of one hundred or more are expressed in figures.

> One faculty member accumulated forty-seven parking tickets during the year, all of which he sent to the dean with elaborate explanations of their injustice.

> The university finally decided to build a new parking lot with space for 175 cars.

26. Dates   Dates may be written in one of two ways:

> December 7, 1941
> 7 December 1941

The important thing is to be consistent and to use the appropriate punctuation. When referring to a month and year, the first form requires a comma and the second does not.

> December, 1941
> December 1941

Under no circumstances is it necessary or permissible to refer to *December of 1941.* The use of a superfluous preposition has become increasingly common, probably because writers are confused about the punctuation of dates and wish to avoid the issue altogether. There is no warrant, however, for this barbarous form.

One sometimes runs across things like "from 1967–72," which should be written either "from 1967 to 1972" or, less felicitously, "the 1967–72 period."

27. Roman Numerals   Roman numerals are rapidly going out of use. They are no longer used, for example, in citing volume numbers of periodicals. "Roman numerals, especially when set in full capital letters, are large, cumbersome, and typographically unpleasant," notes the *Chicago Manual*. Furthermore, "some otherwise literate people cannot count up to C the Roman way."

28. Numerals Designating Footnotes   Numerals in the text designed to indicate footnotes should be placed at the end of a sentence whenever possible. They should follow rather than precede a quotation. Sometimes a dual system of symbols can be used, numbers indicating notes that cite sources (which notes are then placed at the end of the text) and asterisks indicating substantive notes (at the bottom of the page). For the sequence of other symbols used with asterisks, see *Chicago Manual*, par. 12.51.

29. Placement of Footnotes   Footnotes should be typed or printed either at the bottom of the page (still the best practice, and one presumably facilitated by the widespread use of word processors) or at the end of the entire text, never at the end of a chapter. If they are printed at the end of the text, they should be numbered in one of two ways: from 1 to *n*, beginning again with each chapter, or cumulatively, from the beginning to the end of the entire book or dissertation. Cumulative numbering, sometimes used in short books, makes it much easier for readers to consult notes placed at the end of the text. The only objection to this considerate practice is that it makes for long super-numerals in the text itself. One answer to that difficulty is to reduce the number of footnotes—a good idea in any case.

30. Footnote Form   For proper form in footnote references, consult the *Chicago Manual*, ch. 15 ("Notes and Bibliographies").

31. Short Titles in Footnotes   The expressions *loc. cit.* (*loco citato*, in the place cited) and *op. cit.* (*opere citato*, in the work cited), often used in footnotes, should be avoided, since they often force readers to make a tedious backward trek in search of the original reference. Use short titles instead. Even *ibid.* is beginning to give way, in many publishing houses, to a short title—a good thing too, since the disallowance of *ibid.* discourages authors from introducing unnecessary citations. The number of footnotes can often be reduced by grouping several citations in one note instead of providing a separate note for each.

III

Characteristics of Bad Writing

Even the most devoted instructor cannot teach a good style or reduce the elements of style to a set of quickly learned techniques.
We learn to write well, if we ever do, by reading good prose, paying
close attention to our own words, revising relentlessly, and recalling
the connections between written and spoken language. A manual
of this sort can only call attention to some of the characteristics
of bad prose and provide a short list of things to avoid. Further
discussion of these matters can be found in George Orwell's essay,
"Politics and the English Language," in *The Elements of Style*, by
William Strunk, Jr., and E. B. White, and in *The Practical Stylist*,
by Sheridan Baker.

32. Nouns and Verbs   Bad writing relies on nouns and adjectives to carry the thought and relegates verbs to an insignificant role. Verbs signify action and movement, and a sentence built
around a lively verb will tend to generate far more energy than a
sentence that merely piles up nouns, adjectives, and other modifiers. Consider the following example, typical of the dull, noun-
heavy, Germanic prose churned out in such abundance by the
academy.

As we have noted, the general trend of American society has been toward a rapid upgrading in the educational status of the population. This means that, relative to past expectations, with each generation there is increased pressure to educational achievement, often associated with parents' occupational ambitions for their children. To a sociologist this is a more or less classical situation of anomic strain, and the youth-culture ideology which plays down intellectual interests and school performance seems to fit in this context. The orientation of the youth culture is, in the nature of the case, ambivalent, but the anti-intellectual side of the ambivalence tends to be overtly stressed. One of the reasons for the dominance of the anti-school side of the ideology is that it provides a means of protest against adults, who are at the opposite pole in the socialization situation. (*Deplorable*)

33. Forms of *To Be* It would take many pages to explain what ails the foregoing passage (par. 32), but much of the trouble originates in the poverty of verbs. In the whole passage, a single verb—*to be*—appears again and again, in various guises, while other verbs (with a few insignificant exceptions) are rigorously excluded. Note in particular that the writer almost always uses some form of *to be* as the principal verb. When he does use a different verb— usually one almost as characterless as *to be* itself—he makes sure to assign it a merely auxiliary role. His refusal to use active verbs means that every sentence has the same structure: a noun plus some form of *to be* plus another noun, usually surrounded with a top-heavy accumulation of modifying clauses. Such monotony, achieved by denying oneself all the rich resources of our language, might be considered a stylistic feat of sorts, if it were not so obviously the line of least resistance.

A simple corrective would help to improve this and similarly afflicted passages: resort to forms of *to be* only when an arduous search turns up no alternative. In nine sentences out of ten, a better verb can be found, and the entire shape and structure of the sentence will immediately improve once an *is* or *was* or *has been* has made its exit. This advice outranks in importance even the more familiar injunction to avoid the passive voice (par. 34). Like all good advice, however, it should not be followed mindlessly in every case. Sometimes the attempt to replace *to be* may complicate things unnecessarily and destroy an otherwise memorable sentence.

To be or not to be, that is the question. (*Good*)

The search for a more active verb ruins not only the scansion but the sense of this sentence.

The questions arises: to be or not to be. (*Bad*)

The question prompts itself to the troubled mind: to live or die. (*Worse*)

I ask myself: should I go on living or do away with myself? (*No better*)

No rule is automatic in its application.

34. The Passive Voice   Inert, lifeless, and evasive, the passive voice disguises the subject and makes it hard to assign responsibility for an action. Precisely its anonymity endears it to bureaucrats, who wish to avoid responsibility for their decisions.

It was decided that further discussions regarding arms reduction would be counterproductive. (*Bureaucratic*)

The level of radioactive waste is not regarded at the moment as a serious health hazard. (*Bureaucratic*)

The passive voice commends itself to academicians for something of the same reasons. It gives an appearance of detachment and objectivity. Unwilling to risk a straightforward judgment, fearful that even a discriminating judgment will appear as the expression of a merely personal opinion or prejudice, the timid scholar takes refuge in the self-effacement of the passive voice.

> It has been determined that many of our subjects could not give even a rough summary of the Bill of Rights. (*Passive, weak, evasive*)

> First amendment freedoms have been given special emphasis in this study, since it was felt that changes in public opinion would be revealed more clearly in this area. (*Passive*)

> Particular attention should be called to the fact that all of our subjects were given the opportunity to amplify their responses in interviews. (*Passive*)

Note that the passive form of verbs consists of some form of *to be* followed by the past participle. A careful search for forms of *to be* will therefore serve to identify and weed out the passive voice as well. "Begin by suspecting every *is*," Baker writes. "*To be*, itself, frequently ought not to be."

35. Abstract Language   Bad academic writing avoids concrete (literally *solid* or *coalesced*) words and phrases as assiduously as it avoids the active voice, and for the same reason: it seeks to convey an impression of scientific precision, of painfully acquired learning and scholarship, of Olympian detachment from the commonplace facts of everyday life. It prefers *phenomena* to *things* or *events*, *socialization* to *growing up*, *orientation* to *position* or *location*. Abstractions are often indispensable, of course (as are forms of *to be*). Sipped in small amounts, they may even have a slightly intoxicating effect, not inconsistent with verbal clarity. Over-indulgence, however, leads to slurred speech and eventually destroys brain cells.

36. Jargon   Every craft or profession evolves a special terminology of its own, indispensable to its practice, precise, sometimes not a little racy and pungent. A mastery of the appropriate lingo signifies the passage from apprenticeship into full membership in a guild, whether it is deep-sea fishing or brain surgery or scholarship. Since outsiders can make no sense of it, however, jargon kills a general conversation, serving merely to identify the speaker as the possessor of secrets inaccessible to the multitude. Hence the appeal of esoteric terminology—sociological, psychoanalytic, Marxist, structuralist, poststructuralist, behaviorist, legal, or medical—to those who wish to impress others with a display of special learning. If you intend to communicate with readers, instead of merely making a formidable first impression, use ordinary language.

37. Hidden Metaphors   As our language loses touch with its roots in everyday experience, all of us find it more and more difficult to remind ourselves of the metaphorical content of words the concrete content of which has been overlaid by layer on layer of abstraction: *depend* (literally to hang from or hang down); *crux* (cross); *gamut* (the musical scale); *dearth* (famine); *mordant* (biting); *stereotype* (a method of printing); *travail* (labor, especially the labor of childbirth); *pitfall* (a trap for birds and animals and by extension for the unwary); *pithy* (referring originally to the stem of a tree). Failure to listen to metaphorical overtones leads to mixed metaphors, usually with unintentionally comic results: "The violent population explosion has paved the way for new intellectual growth." As Baker notes, this sentence "looks pretty good until you realize that explosions do not pave, and that new vegetation does not grow up through pavement." His own sentence, incidentally, would have benefited from the reminder that *realize* means to make something real, to convert assets into cash, and finally to conceive something vividly as real—not simply to come to an understanding of something. A good speaker listens to his own words, to their sound and to their literal and metaphorical meanings. A bad speaker tries so desperately to hold the floor—often by means of such verbal mannerisms, designed to evoke automatic assent, as "okay?" and "y'know?"—that he remains curiously deaf to his own words. Listen.

Listen also to intended metaphors, as well as to unintended ones. A little goes a long way. The following example from *TV Guide* (via the *New Yorker*) reminds us that metaphors, like chain saws, should be used only by skilled hands.

> A round of raucous, good-humored toasts echoed across Silver Bank as emotions that had been corseted over months of arduous toil rose to the surface and—fueled by champagne—breached.

38. Unnecessary Preliminaries   Instead of explaining what you're about to say, go ahead and say it. Consider these three sentences (the first by Herbert Croly, the second by Charlotte Perkins Gilman, and the third by Thorstein Veblen), which also illustrate a number of other common faults.

> Let it be immediately added, however, that this economic independence and prosperity has [*sic*] always been absolutely associated in the American mind with free political institutions. (*Bad*)

> The fact that, speaking broadly, women have, from the very beginning, been spoken of expressively enough as "the sex," demonstrates clearly that this is the main impression which they have made upon observers and recorders. (*Bad— but good*)

> There seems to be fair ground for saying that the habits of thought fostered by modern industrial life are, on the whole, not favorable to the maintenance of the patriarchal household or to that status of women which the institution in its best development implies. (*Very bad*)

In all three sentences, the trouble begins with an unnecessary introductory phrase, in which the writer hems and haws while trying to figure out what's coming next. Such devices do help to get the juices flowing, but having served that purpose, they should be ruthlessly weeded out in revision. If you've got something broad to say, say it without explanation or apology. If it seems fair to say what you're about to say—and surely it would be wrong to say something deliberately unfair—go ahead and get it out. The same objection applies to the further qualification in the last of these sentences, *on the whole*. If the statement admits of serious exceptions, they had better be discussed. If not, the qualification only indicates indecision, or, in Veblen's case, a certain fussy regard for the worst literary conventions of academic scholarship, which his work defied in so many other ways. More than anything else, however, it is the unrelenting abstractness of Veblen's language that cripples this sentence and makes it difficult, finally, to figure out just what he intends to say—perhaps something like this: *Modern industry undermines the patriarchal household and makes it more and more difficult to keep women in a dependent position.*

As for the first sentence, it never gets off the ground at all. Instead it sinks under its own weight. Note that it contains not one but two passive verbs. The sentence might better read: *Americans have always associated free political institutions with economic independence and prosperity*, or better yet (since *associated* remains noncommittal about the exact nature of the association): *Americans have always seen economic independence and prosperity as an essential precondition of free political institutions.* This last version avoids anticlimax—another point in its favor.

39. Climax and Anti-Climax   Try to arrange sentences so that the most important words or ideas come at the end. The importance of this rule is illustrated by the sentence by Charlotte Perkins Gilman, quoted in par. 38. At the same time, this sentence shows why no rules of this sort can claim to be definitive. Her resort to *the fact that* (an "especially debilitating expression," as noted by Strunk and White) violates an elementary principle of good writing, as does the passive voice introduced by those feeble words. In spite of its ungainliness, however, the sentence has a good deal of force. In this case, we can't get rid of the passive voice without also getting rid of *women* as the subject of this clause, and Gilman clearly intends to emphasize women (both as subjects of the clause and also as objects of certain bad ideas)—not those who entertain false ideas of them. Perhaps the underlying trouble in this sentence, then (as in Croly's sentence, quoted in par. 38), is that it ends in an anti-climax. If this central flaw were corrected, everything else would fall into place: *The main impression women have made on observers and recorders over the centuries appears in the expressive, telltale phrase that has characterized them from the beginning: "the sex."*

40. Parallel Construction, Elegant Variation   The principle of parallel construction, as explained by Strunk and White, "requires that expressions similar in content and function be outwardly similar." Consider this example:

> Abraham Lincoln put the man before the dollar; Reagan puts the dollar first. (*Unobjectionable*)

An inexperienced writer, judging this sentence too repetitious in its structure, might rewrite it:

> Abraham Lincoln put the man before the dollar, but the dollar comes first with Reagan. (*Indecisive*)

Instead of improving the sentence, this change weakens it by literally changing the subject. It illustrates the fallacy of elegant variation, which in its needless attempt to avoid repetition creates uncertainty about just what ideas the writer means to emphasize.

The principle of parallel construction has a more strictly grammatical application. An article or preposition applying to all the terms of a series must appear either before the first term or before each term. Instead of writing *in spring, summer, and in winter*, write either *in spring, summer, and winter* or *in spring, in summer, and in winter.* Here again, elegant variation creates an effect the opposite of elegant.

Since certain words idiomatically require the use of a particular pronoun, the variation of pronouns in compound constructions becomes a grammatical necessity, not just another example of misplaced eloquence.

> She felt both impatience and contempt for her opponents. (*Lacks parallel construction*)

This sentence should be rewritten:

> She felt both impatience with and contempt for her opponents. (*Grammatical but stilted*)

If the rewritten sentence sounds somewhat stilted (and such sentences usually do), it should be revised more drastically:

> Her feelings about her opponents mixed impatience and contempt.

41. Placement of Related Words   Keep related words together.

> An attempt to amend the existing law, which many considered ill-advised, went down to defeat. (*Jumbled*)

Here, as is so often the case, failure to keep related words together creates ambiguity. The reader has no way of knowing whether the law or the proposal to amend it provoked charges of injustice. The following revision would eliminate this ambiguity only by creating another disjuncture.

> An attempt, considered ill-advised by many, to amend the existing law went down to defeat. (*Still jumbled*)

More radical surgery is called for:

An ill-advised attempt to amend the existing law, as many
considered it, went down to defeat.

The second revision manages to connect *ill-advised* and *attempt*
without wrecking the rest of the sentence.

42. Ambiguous and Mismatched Antecedents   Pronouns
refer to earlier nouns, and the failure to clarify their antecedents
creates ambiguity.

Aaron Burr, the grandson of Jonathan Edwards, who was
known to his contemporaries as an infidel and traitor,
emerges in Vidal's novel as a man of consummate political
vision. (*Ambiguous*)

She and her teaching assistants gave such vivid lectures on
the Tsars that her students remembered them for years.
(*Ambiguous*)

Was it Burr or Edwards who was known to his contemporaries as an
infidel and traitor? Did her students remember her and her teaching assistants, their lectures, or the Tsars? In the first example, a rearrangement designed, once again, to keep related words together
(par. 41) will eliminate the ambiguity.

Jonathan Edwards's grandson Aaron Burr, who was known
to his contemporaries as an infidel and traitor, appears in
Vidal's novel as a man of vision.

In the second example, a more drastic rearrangement eliminates
the pronoun all together—the only way to repair this sentence.

Her students remembered for years the vivid lectures she
and her teaching assistants gave on the Tsars.

A pronoun must agree with its antecedent.

General Motors raised their prices across the board. (*Wrong*)

General Motors, a company, is a singular noun and demands a singular pronoun.

> General Motors raised its prices across the board.

The recent fashion of referring to companies in the plural, in the hope of making them appear just plain folks, should be ignored. Do not follow the example of the commercial for Lite Beer, a beverage said to contain

> a third less calories than their regular beer. (*Bad*)

The following example raises the same issue—agreement of pronouns with their antecedents—in a form more difficult to resolve.

> Each of her students hoped to follow their heroine's example. (*Ungrammatical*)

As a singular pronoun, *each* demands another singular pronoun, not the plural *their*. But here we come to a hotly disputed issue. Should it be followed by the generic masculine pronoun? (Let us assume that her students included both men and women.)

> Each of her students hoped to follow his heroine's example.

Or should it be followed by one of the constructions recently favored as a means of overcoming the sexual prejudice allegedly inherent in the generic masculine pronoun?

> Each of her students hoped to follow his or her heroine's example.

> Each of her students hoped to follow his/her heroine's example.

> Each of her students hoped to follow her heroine's example.

We shall not attempt to resolve this issue, except to note that the well-intentioned effort to redress sexual injustices through grammatical reform sometimes leads to slightly ludicrous effects.

In the first edition of *The Pursuit of Loneliness* (1970), Philip Slater described how he came back to America after a long absence abroad and saw his country with new eyes.

> A traveler returning to his own country after spending some time abroad obtains a fresh vision of it. He still wears his traveler's antennae—a sensitivity to nuances of custom and attitude that helps him to adapt and make his way in strange settings.

In the revised edition (1976), Slater conscientiously changed all the masculine pronouns to feminine pronouns, even in this passage, in which he obviously refers to himself in the third person.

> A traveler returning to her own country after spending some time abroad receives a fresh vision of it. She still wears her traveler's antennae—a sensitivity to nuances of custom and attitude that helps her adapt and make her way in strange settings.

It is as if Henry Adams, under the influence of modern feminism, were to rewrite the entire *Education*, beginning with the famous opening lines of the second paragraph:

> Had she been born in Jerusalem under the shadow of the Temple and circumcised in the Synagogues by her uncle the high priest, under the name of Israel Cohen, she would scarcely have been more distinctly branded, and not much more heavily handicapped in the races of the coming century, in running for such stakes as the century was to offer . . .

Considerations of style and grammar must never be allowed to override considerations of common sense.

43. Split Infinitives   These should be avoided, in conformity to the principle that related words should be kept together.

It is better to have loved and lost than to never have loved. (*Wrong*)

This sentence should read:

It is better to have loved and lost than never to have loved. (*Right*)

44. Truncated Infinitives   Sometimes idiomatic usage demands the omission of *to* in an infinitive, as in this sentence:

It made me see things more clearly. (*Idiomatic*)

In the following sentence, however, *to* should have been retained before *establish* (though not before the second infinitive, *maintain*).

In a gender-defined and -dichotomized society, benevolent activities helped women establish and maintain affectional ties with one another. (*Unidiomatic*)

The objection, as always, is not so much to informality as such as to the incongruous mixture of an informal construction—the infinitive without *to*—with the formality, if anything the excessive formality that characterizes so much academic writing, evident here in words and phrases like "gender-defined and -dichotomized," "activities," and "affectional ties."

45. Subject-Verb Disagreement   Verbs must agree in number with their subjects. This sounds simple, but even experienced writers lose track of the number of their subjects, as when Herbert Croly, in the example already quoted (par. 38), says that

economic independence and prosperity has always been absolutely associated . . . with free political institutions. (*Ungrammatical*)

He should have said *have* instead of *has*. For some common pitfalls of this type, see Strunk and White, *The Elements of Style*, 4th edition (2000), pp. 9–10, par. 9.

Sometimes a collective noun takes a plural verb:

The *majority* of professors *have* PhDs.

46. Inconsistent and Inappropriate Verb Tenses   Unless you have a good reason for changing verb tenses, stick to one tense instead of shuttling back and forth from one to another. Use the present tense to refer to events in literature, which remain timeless, and don't be diverted from it by the writer's own use of the past tense. Do not write:

> Normally a teetotaler, Lapham drinks several glasses of wine and begins to brag about his business exploits. The next morning he feared that he had made a fool of himself. (*Unnecessary change of tenses*)

The present tense should be used in the second sentence as well as in the first:

> The next morning he fears that he has made a fool of himself.

Historical events will obviously be described, most of the time, in the past tense, but the present tense may be more appropriate when one refers to commentary on those events.

> In the 1850s, Northern politicians began to insist on the moral dimension of the slavery issue. Lincoln told Alexander Stevens that the whole question boiled down to the North's belief in the evil of slavery, in opposition to the South's belief in its goodness. Historians like Avery Craven think this talk of good and evil was pure demagoguery. Craven argues that slavery should have been treated strictly as a question of expediency, without regard to morality.

In a misguided attempt to liven up writing about past events and to give an otherwise humdrum narrative an air of drama, journalists have become addicted to a construction that combines *would* with a verb in the present tense, in order to anticipate events known to the reader but not to all people living in earlier times. (Perhaps we should call this construction the historical future tense.)

> Much later, ironically, he himself would join the revolutionary movement. (*Portentous*)

Sometimes, in a still more frenzied search for melodramatic effect, the writer uses the present tense for historical narration and then leaps into the future with an "is to," with which he hopes to make us marvel (with the advantage of hindsight) at the way big things grow from little beginnings. ("And that lonely little boy was— Richard Milhous Nixon!") Woody Allen satirizes this narrative style in his comic sketch of the Earl of Sandwich, putative inventor of the sandwich:

> 1738: Disowned, he sets out for the Scandinavian countries, where he spends three years in intensive research on cheese. . . . Upon his return to England, he meet Nell Smallbore, a greengrocer's daughter, and they marry. She is to teach him all he will ever know about lettuce.

Do not resort to such devices in the hope of creating excitement, lest you find yourself the object of satire. Let your ideas generate their own excitement. Even a small detail, accurately observed, is worth any number of historical extravaganzas in the Hollywood style.

47. Dangling Participles and Modifiers   A participle has to modify an appropriate noun, but every writer occasionally changes his mind about the subject of a sentence in mid-course and forgets to change the modifying participles. This lapse can lead to results that are ambiguous and often absurd as well.

Having made this general statement about the growth of patriarchy in the home, one caveat must be entered. (*Dangling participle*)

Having committed himself to a sentence that must have as its subject *I*, *we*, *the author*, or some such expression, the author changes his mind at the last minute, probably because he doesn't after all want to assume responsibility for the *warning* he is about to issue. (*Caveat*, incidentally, is pompous and pretentious; see par. 35, *Abstract Language*.) The sentence should read:

Having made this general statement about the growth of patriarchy in the home, I must enter one warning.

Other modifiers can dangle, not just participles. The following sentence from Ernest Poole's novel *The Harbor* creates a comical effect, since the narrator here recalls himself as a young boy of six or seven.

An enormous woman with heavy eyes, I was in awe of her from the first. (*Dangling modifier*)

Poole has inadvertently made his young protagonist characterize himself as an enormous woman with heavy eyes. What he really meant was:

An enormous woman with heavy eyes, she filled me with awe from the first.

48. Gerunds Incorrectly Modified   A gerund is a participle used as a noun; for example, *Parting is such sweet sorrow*. As a noun, it must be accompanied, when it is accompanied at all, by a possessive noun or pronoun, not by a noun or pronoun in the objective case. In the following pairing, the incorrect sentence can be spotted without difficulty.

Shakespeare devotes almost a whole scene to them parting. (*Wrong*)

Shakespeare devotes almost a whole scene to their parting. (*Right*)

Other mistakes of the kind, however, often pass without notice.

Our teachers objected to us raising any questions at all. (*Wrong*)

She couldn't stand Fred drinking. (*Wrong*)

We relished them singing old Baptist hymns. (*Wrong*)

In each of these sentences, the writer should have stopped to ask what was the object (or indirect object) of the verb. In the second sentence, for example, it wasn't Fred she couldn't stand but Fred's drinking. In each case, the verbal noun should be modified by a possessive noun or pronoun.

Our teachers objected to our raising any questions at all. (*Right*)

She couldn't stand Fred's drinking. (*Right*)

We relished their singing old Baptist hymns. (*Right*)

Sometimes it is difficult to distinguish between a gerund and a present participle. The point, however, is to provide the appropriate grammatical accompaniment. If the word is a gerund, it needs to be modified by a possessive pronoun.

We admired the girl playing. (*Participle*)

We admired the girl's playing. (*Gerund*)

49. Incomplete and Inappropriate Comparisons A comparative must be used to make an explicit comparison, not just to give a vague impression of comparison.

I can see better with my new glasses. (*Incomplete*)

Better than what? Better than I can see without them? Better than someone else could see *with* them? The reader wants to know exactly what is being compared.

It is because the conjunction *than* introduces a comparison that it should not be used with *different* (*q.v.*, below). The observation that two things differ means precisely that they cannot be compared. Grammarians object to *different than* not, as the *Random House Dictionary* speculates, because the expression is a "solecism" (a breach of good manners) but because it introduces an inappropriate comparison.

Elephants are bigger than ants. (*Correct*)

Elephants are different than ants. (*Incorrect*)

The first sentence compares elephants and ants with reference to a characteristic they have in common, size. Because the second sentence emphasizes what distinguishes them from each other, the use of *than*, which implies common traits susceptible to comparison, becomes inappropriate.

Note also the vagueness that so often attends the false comparison signified by *different than*. Yes, elephants differ from ants, but this observation by itself is not terribly illuminating. In what do they differ and what traits do they share?

Random House—in general an unreliable authority, nowhere more unreliable than in this particular instance—maintains that even difference has degrees and that the adjective, therefore, can be used in the comparative form, as in this sentence:

He is more different than you are. (*Meaningless*)

This sentence hardly clinches the case. Indeed, it does not seem to make any sense at all.

IV

Words Often Misused

For somewhat similar but more extensive lists, see Strunk and White, *The Elements of Style*, 4th edition (2000), pp. 39–65, and Sheridan Baker, *The Practical Stylist*, 6th edition (1985), pp. 246–78.

access   Not to be used as a verb.

accrue   An intransitive verb meaning (1) to accumulate or (2) to come to someone by way of increase or advantage; not to be used as a transitive verb.

How did the state accrue so much power? (*Incorrect*)

Interest on this deposit will begin to accrue immediately. (*Correct*).

According to some theorists, power will accrue to those who control the means of communication. (*Correct*)

adverbs   The suffix *ly* does not automatically create an adverb. A number of adjectives end in *ly*: *gingerly*, *leisurely*. These words should not be used as adverbs, though they often are.

They proceeded at a leisurely pace. (*Not*: They proceeded leisurely to their destination.)

She picked up the rare book in a gingerly manner. (*Not*: She gingerly picked up the rare book.)

The most important word in this category is *likely*, an adjective now widely used, incorrectly, as an adverb. In the sentence,

The senior class voted Baletnikoff the graduate student most likely to succeed,

where the adjective *likely* modifies the noun *graduate*, the word is used correctly. In the following sentence, it is used incorrectly as an adverb.

Baletnikoff will likely succeed. (*Ungrammatical*)

Here the word should be replaced by a real adverb like *probably* or by the adverbial phrase, *in all likelihood*.

Many short adverbs are adverbs already without the addition of *ly*: *so, as, hence, thus*. One sometimes comes across *thusly*, even in newspapers and magazines—a grotesque absurdity.

affect, effect When used as verbs, these words are often confused. *To affect* means to influence; *to effect* means to bring something about, to achieve or accomplish some objective.

Voters' choices can *effect* [not *affect*] minor changes and even *affect* [not *effect*] major policy decisions.

albeit A pretentious literary word much in vogue. Use *though* or *although*.

an The article *an* should be used before words beginning with a vowel sound, and under no other circumstances. Do not write *an historical* or *an utopian*—affected literary mannerisms. The sound, not the spelling, determines the article. We say *an honor*, not *a honor*. Here again, it is important to listen to the sound of words, not just to look at them on paper or on the screen of a word processor.

ascribe, subscribe   Sometimes confused, as in:

Gramsci *ascribed* to the idea that history is the story of class conflict. (*Incorrect*)

To ascribe means to attribute, impute, or assign. *To subscribe* means, among other things, to assent to or agree with.

Gramsci *subscribed* to the idea. (*Correct*)

Gramsci *ascribed* to class conflict a leading role in history. (*Correct*)

author   Not to be used as a verb, as in: *She authored one of the standard works on the subject.* Use *wrote*.

behaviors   We owe this monstrosity to clinical and behavioral psychology, one of the most fruitful sources of contemporary jargon (see par. 36). The word is especially objectionable in the plural, but even in the singular it should be avoided. *Behavior* should never be used as a synonym for *conduct* or *action*. Confine it to its original meaning (which was derived from biology, not psychology): an organism's regular and predictable response to a stimulus. The word also means *deportment*, in which sense it used to be a favorite of elementary school teachers. This meaning, however, has gone the way of the one-room schoolhouse.

bewildering variety   A cliché (*q.v.*, below). Never use either *bewildering* or *infinite* as an accompaniment to *variety*. Think of something new.

but   Not to be used as a synonym for *only*, as in: *He had but one life to give for his country.* This usage is pretentious and literary (though ubiquitous, alas). For another and far better use of *but*, see *however*.

clichés   Bad writing relies heavily on ready-made phrases. "Modern writing at its worst," Orwell notes, "consists in gumming together long strips of words which have already been set in order by someone else." This method of writing requires less effort than original thought, but it provides readers with neither delight nor instruction. Learn to recognize clichés—*bewildering variety, infinite variety, lasting impression, fraught with difficulty, part and parcel*—and ruthlessly weed them out.

competence, competency   Fowler (*Modern English Usage*) urges confining the first form to the senses of *ability* and legal capacity and the second to the sense of modest means. Concerning the large class of doubtful cases, where it is unclear whether *ce* or *cy* is the correct form, he makes a couple of helpful observations: that shorter sounding words (*frequent*) usually take *cy* (*frequency*) and longer sounding ones (*innocent*) *ce* (*innocence*), and that many words take *ce* in the singular and *cies*, rather than *ces*, in the plural (*irrelevance, irrelevancies*). See also *dependence, dependency*.

complement   Not to be confused with *compliment*. To *compliment* is to praise; to *complement* is to fill up or complete, to supply a deficiency or make up a complete set.

comprise   A somewhat prettified and much overused word meaning *to include* or *contain*, literally *to embrace*. As a fancy word, it is best avoided, especially since it is almost always used incorrectly. Strunk and White provide a useful illustration of the word's correct use: "A zoo comprises mammals, reptiles, and birds (because it 'embraces,' or 'includes,' them. But animals do not comprise ('embrace') a zoo—they constitute a zoo." Before using this word (if you must use it at all), always remember its literal meaning: *embrace*.

confide Even otherwise careful writers find it hard to refer to the act of writing in a diary without using this cliché: *Adams confided to his diary that he coveted the presidency.* Use another verb.

convince Should be followed by a clause introduced by *that*, never by an infinitive. *She convinced her son to study the piano* is incorrect. Write something like: *She convinced her son that he should study the piano.*

continual, continuous Often confused. A *continuous* action or motion goes on without interruption. *Continual*, on the other hand, implies an indefinitely recurring series.

criterion The plural is *criteria*; see *Greek and Latin plurals.*

critique Not to be used as a verb.

dearth A literary word meaning *famine, scarcity.* Avoid it.

dependence, dependency According to Fowler, *dependence* should be used when the word is used abstractly (as when speaking of the harvest's *dependence* on the weather or a child's *dependence* on his parents), while *dependency* should be reserved for the "concrete sense of a thing that depends upon or is subordinate to another," as in the British colonial dependencies. This is not an easy distinction to make. In general, the first form should be preferred.

desire Do not use the verb *desire* when you mean simply *wish* or *want*, as in: *He desired the girls to go to the game.* (*Unnecessarily formal*)

different Should be followed by *from*, not *than* (see par. 49, *Incomplete and Inappropriate Comparisons*).

dilemma   Sometimes misspelled, curiously, as *dilemna*, perhaps on the false analogy of *alumna*; almost invariably misused to refer to any problem or perplexity. *Dilemma* refers to a choice between equally attractive or equally undesirable alternatives and should be restricted to this meaning alone.

disinterested   Not to be confused with *uninterested*. *Disinterested* signifies impartiality or an absence of any considerations of personal advantage; *uninterested* signifies boredom or indifference. Why does *disinterested* almost invariably show up, these days, when the speaker means *uninterested*? Probably because it sounds a little more imposing. Since most writers no longer know what *disinterested* means, they prefer it for that very reason, as a high-sounding substitute for the commonplace word designating boredom. Remember that disinterested inquiry—the ideal of scholarship—refers not to investigations conducted in a state of apathy or indifference but to a pursuit of truth so intense that it refuses to allow personal whim or inclination to interfere with the determination to follow an idea wherever it may lead. Disinterested inquiry signifies a refusal to indulge in wishful thinking.

due to the fact that   Use *because*. See also *fact*.

effect   See *affect*.

enormity   Refers not to size but to wickedness.

The corporation's enormity puts it beyond effective public control. (*Wrong*)

The enormity of his crime appalled even the hardened cynics on death row. (*Right*)

enthuse   Too cute for words.

exploitative   Many writers prefer the superfluous syllable to the simpler adjective *exploitive*, evidently on the assumption that scholarly writing calls for as many syllables as possible. The longer form also evinces a tell-tale preference for nouns over verbs; faced with a choice between building an adjective on the verb *exploit* or on the noun *exploitation*, the wordy writer instinctively chooses the noun. See *interpretative*; see also par. 32, *Nouns and Verbs*.

fact   A good word, rightly beloved of historians, except when it appears in the phrase *the fact that*. Prune away this lazy expression; its elimination always leads to an immediate improvement in any sentence.

factor   Another word much used by historians, but not a good one. It is vague and indecisive. Use something more direct, specific, and idiomatic.

feel   Too often used to mean *think*—another sign of the infiltration of ordinary speech by psychobabble. Say *think*, not *feel*, when you mean think.

finalize   It is easy to coin verbs endlessly from nouns and adjectives simply by adding *ize*. But this practice merely contributes to the noun-adjective glut, to the growing dependence on nouns and adjectives instead of verbs (see par. 32, *Nouns and Verbs*). A verb coined in this lazy way contributes nothing to clear and vigorous speech, and this particular example is one of the worst.

firstly, secondly   *First* and *second* can serve as adverbs without the addition of *ly*, which is unnecessary and pretentious.

fraught   Becomes a cliché when used with *difficulty* or, indeed, with most nouns.

Greek and Latin plurals   Words ending in *on* or *un*, like *criterion*, *phenomenon*, *dictum*, and *medium*, form the plural by adding *a* to the stem: *criteria*, *phenomena*, *dicta*, *media*. The form ending in *a* is never the singular.

> The number of publications is a poor *criteria* of scholarly achievement. (*Wrong*)

> The number of publications is a poor *criterion*. (*Right*)

> The *dicta* that the *media* is the message serves as the cornerstone of McLuhan's system. (*Wrong*)

> The *medium* is the message: such is McLuhan's *dictum*. (*Right*)

historical   See *an*.

hopefully   Constantly misused, as in

> Hopefully I'll finish my paper before the end of the term. (*Terrible*)

The writer appears to mean:

> I hope I'll finish my paper before the end of the term.

What she said, however, was:

> I'll finish my paper, in a hopeful spirit, by the end of the term.

It is hard to account for the enormous appeal of this silly little construction. It probably helps to de-emphasize the subject, to shift attention from the actor to circumstances beyond one's control. In the foregoing example, the writer seems to suggest that whether or not she finishes her paper is something over which she herself has no control. What she really means, perhaps, is something like this:

I hope that things will somehow work out so that my paper gets finished by the end of the term.

host of Comes under the ban on fancy phrases and clichés. Say *many*.

however This eminently useful word becomes obnoxious, and often downright ungrammatical, when used where a simple *but* would suffice.

He wanted to come to school, however he just couldn't make it. (*Bad*)

Guided by a preference for polysyllables over the simple conjunction *but*, this writer (the same writer, in all likelihood, who habitually uses *desire* instead of *want*) has produced a grammatical monstrosity. If he insists on using *however*, he should at least revise the punctuation:

He wanted to come; however, he just couldn't make it. (*Not much better*)

This version is grammatical but still deplorable, not only because it incongruously mixes formal speech (*however*) with colloquialism (*just couldn't make it*) but because *however* always makes an awkward, stilted, and pompous effect when placed at the beginning of a clause or sentence. Introduce it into the middle of a sentence, surrounded by commas.

The French revolution began as an uprising of nobles against the crown. Representatives of the third estate, however, soon turned it to their own purposes.

If you want to begin a sentence by contradicting the last, use *but* instead of *however*.

impact   Do not use as a verb (see par. 32, *Nouns and Verbs*).

imply, infer   Constantly confused nowadays. To *imply* is to speak indirectly or hint; to *infer* is to deduce or guess at.

Ziegler's statement that his earlier statements were "inoperative" implied that they contained any number of lies. (*Correct*)

Most commentators inferred that his earlier statements were deliberate falsifications. (*Correct*)

import   As a noun, this word usually refers to purpose, meaning, or significance, not to importance. When Byron referred to *words of dubious import*, he meant that their meaning was doubtful and ambiguous, not that they had no importance.

in terms of   Jettison this excess baggage.

Plato and Aristotle were the most important of ancient philosophers in terms of their subsequent influence. (*Wordy and vague*)

Their influence over the subsequent development of Western thought makes Plato and Aristotle the most important of ancient philosophers. (*Better*)

interface   Not to be used as a verb; to be avoided even as a noun.

infinite variety   See *clichés*, above.

interpretative   *Interpretive* is better; see *exploitative*, above.

its   The possessive form of *it*, not to be confused with the contraction *it's*, where the apostrophe stands for the missing *i* (see par. 10, *Apostrophes in Contractions*).

The party reached *it's* climax in a shower of shattered champagne glasses. (*Wrong*)

The party reached *its* climax. (*Right*)

Its going to be a lovely day tomorrow. (*Wrong*)

It's going to be a lovely day. (*Right*)

Contractions should usually be avoided altogether in formal writing; see par. 10.

lay, lie   *Lay* is the past tense of the intransitive verb *to lie.*

Dogs often turn three times in a circle before they *lie* down.

As soon as he heard thunder, my dog *lay* down under the bed.

Lay is also, unfortunately, the present tense of the transitive verb meaning *put* or *place.* The past tense of this verb is *laid*, not *lay.*

When you build a house, you first *lay* a proper foundation. (*Present tense*)

Before building the rest of the house, they *laid* the foundation. (*Past tense*)

Spiders and hens *lay* eggs in abundance but otherwise have little in common. (*Present tense*)

Stalin *laid* his cards on the table. (*Past tense*)

lead, led   *Lead* (pronounced *leed*) is the present tense of the verb meaning *guide* or *conduct.* The past tense of this verb is *led*, not *lead* (pronounced *led*). The confusion evidently arises from the noun *lead* (a heavy metal), the pronunciation of which, unfortunately, is identical with the past tense of *lead.*

Anyone whose ideas about America derived solely from *Dallas* would conclude that most Americans *lead* an exciting life, surrounded by enormous affluence. (*Present tense of the verb*)

Vergil *led* Dante through the underworld and explained everything they saw. (*Past tense*)

Most cars now require gasoline that contains no *lead*. (*Noun*)

less, fewer   *Less* refers to quantity, *fewer* to number. The advertising slogan proclaiming that Lite Beer has a "third less calories than their regular beer" is objectionable not only because it falsely personalizes the Miller Brewing Company (see par. 42, *Ambiguous and Mismatched Antecedents*), but because it uses *less* when it should use *fewer*. As one of William Safire's correspondents points out, dietary beers "can have less body, less foam, less taste, less color, and they can be less filling, less fattening and less expensive, but they can have only *fewer* calories."

life style   The appeal of this tired but now ubiquitous phrase probably lies in its suggestion that life is largely a matter of style. Find something else to say about life.

like, as   The use of *like* as a conjunction is ungrammatical. The ungrammatical use of *like*, now widespread, achieved prominence in a banal advertising slogan designed to counter the first medical reports linking smoking to cancer:

Winston tastes good *like* a cigarette should. (*Incorrect*)

In subsequent advertisements, Winston continued its campaign to establish smoking as a kind of honorable American folkway by making fun of the pedants and purists who insisted, correctly but irrelevantly, that good grammar requires:

Winston tastes good, *as* a cigarette should. (*Correct*)

In this form, of course, the slogan would have failed to carry the reassurance conveyed by ungrammatical speech: the implicit message that smoking remains, notwithstanding medical disapproval, as American as apple pie and sloppy grammar.

Even Webster, usually permissive in such matters, frowns on *like* as a conjunction, but only after illustrating its use by a line from Keats:

> They raven down scenery *like* children do sweetmeats. (*Ungrammatical but clear and vivid*)

likely   Not to be used as an adverb; see *adverbs*, above.

loan, lend   *Loan* is the noun; *lend*, the verb.

> If you *loan* me twenty dollars, I'll pay you back as soon as I can. (*Wrong*)

> If you *lend* me the money, I'll repay the *loan* with interest. (*Right*)

Webster now countenances *loan* as a verb. This usage remains objectionable, however, not because it is colloquial but because its widespread use encourages the general tendency to replace verbs with nouns and to make nouns do the work of more active parts of speech.

ly   For the use of this suffix, see *adverbs*, above.

meaningful   Usually a meaningless word, as in *meaningful experience, meaningful relationship, meaningful dialogue.*

medium   Plural, *media.* See *Greek and Latin plurals*, above.

myriad   Write *many* instead of *a myriad.*

nostalgia   This word, which originally means *homesickness*, is now used so loosely that it has become almost meaningless, for example:

> Such hand craftsmanship seems as nostalgic now as the pre-Depression optimism that is memorialized in carved wood and stone.

The writer preferred *nostalgic* to *outdated, obsolete, forgotten,* or some other direct word for reasons that are too complicated to analyze in a short space. Whatever they are, they obviously do not include clear thinking about the past.

orientate   Not to be used as a substitute for *orient*.

part and parcel   Cliché (*q.v.,* above)

phenomenon   Plural, *phenomena*; see *Greek and Latin plurals*. See also par. 35, *Abstract Language*.

plethora   Highfalutin substitute for *superabundance* or *excess*. Don't use it.

point in time   The Watergate hearings popularized this obnoxious bit of bureaucratese. Say *at that time*, not *at that point in time*. *Point* adds only the rhetorical illusion of precision.

preclude   This verb, much misused, takes as its object only things, never persons. Its misuse arises from the wish to find an elegant variation for *prevent*.

> Circumstances *precluded* me from finishing my paper. (*Incorrect*)

> Circumstances *prevented* me from finishing. (*Correct*)

The short time allotted to commentators precluded a searching discussion. (*Correct*)

predominate   An intransitive verb meaning *to rule* or *prevail*, often confused with the adjective *predominant*, meaning *foremost* or *overriding*.

Japan is the predominate industrial country in Asia. (*Incorrect*)

According to some alarmists, Japan will soon become the predominant industrial country in the whole world. (*Correct*)

prestigious   A recent coinage of no value. Even Webster refused until recently to list it.

preventative   There is no such word. Take out the extra syllable: *preventive*. See *exploitative, interpretative.*

principal, principle   Often confused. As an adjective, *principal* is highest, chief, main; hence, as a noun, it refers to a chief, leader, or head (also to a sum of money lent at interest). *Principle*, which is never an adjective, refers to a fundamental truth or tenet, a basic doctrine, an axiom or law. Schoolteachers used to explain the difference by insisting that the *principal* of the school was a *pal*.

Channing's *principal* objection to Calvinism is a moral objection: that it fails to make people good. (*Correct*)

The *principle* underlying Channing's thought is that God arranges things for the happiness and convenience of human beings. (*Correct*)

prior to   Elegant variation for *before*. Avoid it.

privilege   Not to be used as a verb.

problem   Much overused, and misused as well, as a synonym for any kind of trouble, difficulty, mishap, obstacle, or misfortune — probably in conformity with the national belief that every untoward or unexpected turn of events has a simple solution. The word also appeals to insecure writers as a euphemistic form of criticism, as in the headline:

Problems Mar RPO Concert. (*Euphemistic*)

Many writers seem to think that *problem* gives less offense than a more straightforward account of the trouble — in this case, that the soloist lost her place and nearly brought the whole performance to a halt. Finally, the word also serves as a refuge for writers who wish to express disagreement without ruffling any feathers.

I have problems with your argument. (*Evasive and euphemistic*)

Instead of saying that the argument is wrong, the speaker manages to suggest that the fault somehow lies with himself. Misguided considerations of tact should give way to clarity. Confine the word to its original meaning: a question proposed for solution.

quote   Not to be used as a noun. The noun is *quotation*.

relate   Elegant variation for *say* (*q.v.*, below). Also a particularly repellant bit of psychobabble indicating rapport.

say   Averse to this direct and simple word, many writers will go to any length to avoid it: *opine, state, hazard, confide, sneer, declare, relate, observe, exclaim,* and so on. Don't.

separate   Note the spelling; not *seperate*. School teachers used to point out that *a rat* lurked in this word: a pointless but effective mnemonic device.

tack, tact   These words are sometimes confused:

> After failing to subdue Pamela by force, Mr. B. decides to try a new *tact*. (*Incorrect and unintentionally amusing*)

Tact, from the Latin for *touch*, refers to delicacy and social grace. *Tack*, a sailing term, refers to the ship's course or direction.

that   Watch out for the double *that*:

> We're hoping *that* by meeting with our congressman and our senators *that* the administration will give this issue the top priority that it deserves. (*Hopelessly muddled*)

The second *that* is superfluous—usually a sign of tangled syntax, as here, where *meeting*, originally intended to modify *we*, ends up modifying *the administration* instead (see. par. 47, *Dangling Participles and Modifiers*).

that, which   The subject of vast confusion. It will not do to change every *that* to a *which*—a corrective feat one instructor reported with an air of accomplishment. The use of these relative pronouns depends on the grammatical context. *Which* is used in a nonrestrictive clause (that is, a parenthetical clause that does not serve to define a noun or to distinguish it from other nouns in the same category but appears instead simply as an afterthought). *That* is used in a restrictive clause (a clause making a defining, limiting, or qualifying statement about the noun it modifies).

> Veblen's social theory, which appealed to reform-minded engineers, rested on a distinction between business and industry.

In this sentence, the clause introduced by *which* does not limit or define or restrict the meaning of *social theory*. It merely adds something to it. Its being nonrestrictive in effect makes the clause paren-

thetical, and that is why it is set off by commas, like other parenthetical phrases (see par. 2, *Breathing Spaces*).

> The ideas *that* appealed to reform-minded engineers
> stressed the distinction between business and industry.

Here, by contrast, the clause introduced by *that* limits, defines, and
restricts the meaning of *ideas*. The sentence refers not just to any
ideas but specifically to those appealing to engineers. Because the
restrictive clause limits and defines the preceding noun, the punctuation integrates it into the sentence instead of setting it off by
commas.

Strictly speaking, the punctuation, not the use of *which* and
that, distinguishes a restrictive from a nonrestrictive clause (best
thought of, again, as parenthetical or nonessential). The use of
which is mandatory in nonrestrictive clauses.

> Veblen's theory, *that* appealed to reform-minded engineers,
> rested on a distinction between business and industry. (*In-*
> *correct*)

The use of *that* is not mandatory, on the other hand, in restrictive
clauses. Nevertheless it should be strongly favored as more idiomatic and less labored. The recent popularity of *which* derives precisely from a feeling that it is a shade more formal and pompous
than *that*—a good reason for the careful writer, as opposed to the
merely pompous and pretentious writer, to prefer *that*, whenever a
choice presents itself.

this   Often used without a clearly specified antecedent,
especially at the beginning of a sentence.

> Galileo demonstrated that the earth moves around the sun,
> not vice versa. This changed the way people thought about
> man's place in the cosmos.

It may be pedantic to ask whether *this* refers to *the sun, vice versa,* or what, since the context shows clearly enough that it refers to the whole thought contained in the preceding sentence. Nevertheless it is almost always easy to change such a construction into something more forceful, say:

This information changed the way people thought . . .

thus far Elegant substitute for *so far*, much in vogue. Shun it.

thusly Grotesque; see *adverbs*, above.

time frame Another pretentious way of referring to time; see *point in time*, above. *Frame* adds absolutely nothing.

track, tract Beginners sometimes confuse these:

They followed a *tract* in the snow. (*Wrong*)

A *tract* is a short treatise; also an area, expanse, or region. A *track* is a path or way, or a mark left by something that has passed.

traditional, traditionally Like *nostalgia, problem*, and *dilemma*, these words have undergone a journalistic inflation of their meaning, to the point where the adverb, in particular, now conveys no more than the sense of *usually*. "The Monday night football games," we read in a local newspaper, "traditionally draw only a small audience." *Tradition*, which derives from the Latin word for *transmit* or *deliver*, refers to something handed down from the past, not just to an event that recurs more than once. Nor should it be confused with *convention*, which signifies agreement or accepted usage but not necessarily something sanctioned by the authority of the past. Strictly speaking, tradition refers to the transmission of beliefs, customs, or rules, especially by word of mouth, from generation to generation. Even its more vague and general meaning refers to immemorial usage. Conventions come and go; traditions hang on tenaciously.

very   Try to get along without this crutch; you will find that most sentences can easily walk without it.

V

Words Often Mispronounced

anyway Not *anyways*

congratulations One now usually hears *congradulations*, since Americans find that it takes too much effort to pronounce a *t*. Make the effort, here and anywhere else it is required.

ei, ie (in German names) In German, the diphthong *ei* is pronounced *eye*, and *ie* is pronounced *ee*. Since these combinations appear in many proper names, it is essential to get them straight. Thus the American historian was Karl *Schriftgiesser* (Shrift'-geeser), not Shrift'-guyser (or Shrift'-geyser).

et cetera Not *ex* cetera.

eu (in German names). Pronounced *oy*, as in *Reuters* (Roy'-ters).

evidently Accented on the first syllable, like the adjective from which it derives, not on the third syllable.

exquisite Accented on the first syllable, not the second.

fief Rhymes with *beef*, not with *knife*.

flaccid *Flak'-sid*, not *flassid* or *flak-seed*

Foucault *Foo-kowe'*, not *Foo-Kawlt*.

grovel Rhymes with *hovel*, not with *novel*.

Huizinga In Dutch, the *ui* diphthong is pronounced *ow*, as in the illuminated red sign that marks an exit in theaters: *Uit*. Hence, *How'-zinga*, not *Hoy'-zinga*.

inherent in-*hear'*-unt, not in-*hair'*-unt.

laissez faire *Less-ay* faire, not *lah-zay* faire.

luxury Pronounce the *x*: don't say *lugszhury*.

Marcuse *Mar-koo'-zuh*, not Mar-kewz. Cf. *Nietzsche*.

mischievous Sometimes mispronounced with an extra syllable: *mis-chee'-vee-us*. Should be *mis'-chi-vus*.

mnemonic *Nuh-mon'-ic*, not *mem-non-ic*.

Monroe Everywhere except in Rochester, this is pronounced *Mun-ro'*, not *Monn-ro'*.

Nietzsche Neet'-chuh, not *Neetsch* or *Neet-chee*

nostalgia Model the middle syllable on *stallion*, not on *stall*.

nuclear Gives presidents fits: *noo-kew-ler* (Eisenhower);

noo-kee-er (Carter). Should be pronounced the way it looks: *noo-klee-er*.

papal   *Pay'-pul*, not *papp'-ul*.

vice versa   Not *visa versa*.

VI

Proofreaders' Marks

Good writing demands painstaking revision at every stage of composition; this may be the most important requirement of all. The only way to gauge a piece of writing's effect on the reader is to read it over yourself, not once but many times, and to make whatever changes seem called for—for example, to weed out all those unnecessary preliminaries (see par. 38) that help writers to organize their own thoughts but get in the reader's way.

The process of revision requires, among other things, familiarity with the typographical symbols and proofreaders' marks in common use. In the following list, the symbols on the left are usually written in the margins of a typescript or proof, where they will be sure to attract attention. The symbols on the right, after the slash, appear in the text itself. Where only one symbol appears, the same symbol is used in the margins and in the text.

#	Insert space
¶/L	Begin a new paragraph
℘	Delete

stet /·····   Let it stand; restore deleted words. (In the text, the words in question should be underlined with dots.)

cap / ≡   Capitalize

l. c. /   Change capital letter to lower case. (In the text, the letter in question is indicated by a vertical line drawn through the letter—not to be confused with the symbol for deletion.)

◯   Delete space; close up (horizontal)

( )   Delete space; close up (vertical)

tr / ⊔⊓   Transpose words or letters

—ᵢ— m   Insert dash

=   Insert hyphen

run in / ⅂   Run in; run paragraphs together

⊐   Move right

⊏   Move left

ʌ   Insert comma

v̓   Insert apostrophe

v̎   v̎   Insert quotation marks

⊙   Period

Index

Italics indicate entries in Parts IV and V.

abbreviations, 68–69
abstractions, 78
access, 93
accrue, 93
acronyms, 69–70
adjectives, 75
adverbs, 93–94
affect, effect, 94
albeit, 94
an, 94–95
antecedents, 84–86, 110–11
anyway, 113
apostrophes: in contractions, 60; and *it's*, 102; in possessives, 58–59
articles, in a series, 82–83
as, 104–5
ascribe, subscribe, 95
asterisks, and footnotes, 72
author, 95

behaviors, 95
bewildering variety, 95
but, 95–96. See also *however*

capitalization, 70–71; and quotation, 65
clichés, 95, 96, 99, 101, 102, 106
climax and anticlimax, 81–82
commas: as breathing spaces, 55–56; in compound sentences, 56–57; in dates, 71; in relative clauses, 57; in a series, 55; with quotation marks, 57–58
comparisons, 91–92
competence, competency, 96
complement, compliment, 96
composition, principles of, 45–53
compound predicates, 56–57
compound sentences, 56–57, 83
compound words, 61–62
comprise, 96
conclusions, 52–53
confide, 97
congratulations, 113
continual, continuous, 97
contractions, 60–61, 103. See also *its, it's*
convince, 97
criterion, 97. *See also* plurals, Greek and Latin
critique, 97

dangling modifiers, 89–90
dangling participles, 89–90
dashes, 68
dates, 71
dearth, 97
dependence, dependency, 97

desire, 97
different, 97
dilemma, 98
diphthongs, 113, 114
disinterested, 98
due to the fact that, 98

effect, 94
elegant variation, 82–83, 107, 108, 111
ellipses: in quotations, 66
enormity, 98
enthuse, 98
et cetera, 113
euphemism, 108
evidently, 113
exploitative, 99
exquisite, 113

fact, 99
factor, 99
feel, 99
fewer, 104
fief, 114
finalize, 99
firstly, secondly, 99
flaccid, 114
footnotes: form of, 72; *ibid.* in, 73;
    numbering of, 72; placement of,
    72; textual markers to, 72; titles
    in, 72–73
foreign words, 67
fraught, 99

gerunds, 90–91
grovel, 114

historical, 100
hopefully, 100–101
host of, 101
however, 101. See also *but*
hyphens: in compound words,
    61–62; in proper nouns, 62

impact, 102
imply, infer, 102
import, 102
in terms of, 102
infer, 102
infinite variety, 102
infinitives: split, 86–87; truncated,
    87
inherent, 114
initials. *See* acronyms
interface, 102
interpretative, 102
introductions, 45–46, 51–52
italics: for emphasis, 67; and foreign
    words, 67; in quotations, 66; and
    titles, 67
its, it's, 102

jargon, 78–79, 95

laissez faire, 114
lay, lie, 103
lead, led, 103–4
lend, 105
less, 104
life style, 104
like, as, 104–5
likely, 105
loan, 105
luxury, 114
-ly, 105

meaningful, 105
medium, 105. *See also* plurals, Greek
    and Latin
metaphors, 79–80
mischievous, 114
mnemonic, 114
myriad, 105

nostalgia, 106, 114
nouns, 75–77

nuclear, 114–15
numbers, 71

orientate, 106

papal, 115
parallel construction, 82–83
part and parcel, 106
passive voice, 77–78, 80–82
past tense, 88–89
phenomenon, 106. *See also* plurals,
    Greek and Latin
plethora, 106
plurals, 58–59; Greek and Latin, 100
point in time, 106
possessives, 58–60; and *it*, 102
preclude, prevent, 106–7
predominant, predominate, 107
prepositions: in a series, 82–83
present tense, 88–89
prestigious, 107
prevent, 106–7
preventative, 107
principal, principle, 107
prior to, 107
privilege, 107
problem, 108
pronouns: agreement of, 84–85;
    antecedents of, 84–85; in com-
    pound sentences, 83; generic
    masculine, 85–86; and gerunds,
    90–91
proofreaders' marks, 117–18
punctuation. *See* apostrophes; com-
    mas; dashes; ellipses; hyphens;
    quotation marks; semicolons

quotations, 62–66; alterations to, 66;
    indented (block), 65–66; within
    quotations, 64–65
quotation marks, 62–66; with com-

mas, 57; double, 62–64; excessive
    use of, 66–67; and footnote num-
    bers, 72; with semicolons, 57;
    single, 62–64
quote, 108

relate, 108
revision, 117
Roman numerals, 71–72

say, 108
secondly, 99
semicolons: in compound sentences,
    57; with quotation marks, 57–58
separate, 108
split infinitives, 86–87
subscribe, 95
subject-verb agreement, 87–88

tack, tact, 108–9
that, 109
that, which, 109–10
this, 110–11
thus far, 111
thusly, 111
time frame, 111
to be, 76–77, 78
track, tract, 111
traditional, traditionally, 111

unnecessary preliminaries, 80–81, 117

verbs, 75–77; tenses of, 88–89. *See
    also* passive voice; subject-verb
    agreement
very, 111
vice versa, 115

which, 109–10
word division, 68
word placement, 83–84